HOW TO BE
HEADHUNTED

howtobooks

For full details, please send for a free copy of the
latest catalogue to:
How To Books
Spring Hill House, Spring Hill Road
Begbroke, Oxford OX5 1RX, United Kingdom
info@howtobooks.co.uk
www.howtobooks.co.uk

HOW TO BE HEADHUNTED

The insider's guide to making
executive search work for you

John Purkiss & Barbara Edlmair

howtobooks

Every effort has been made to identify and acknowledge the
sources of the material quoted throughout this book. The authors
and publishers apologise for any errors or omissions, and would
be grateful to be notified of any corrections that should appear in
any reprint or new edition.

Published by How To Books Ltd
Spring Hill House, Spring Hill Road
Begbroke, Oxford OX5 1RX, United Kingdom
Tel: (01865) 375794. Fax: (01865) 379162
email: info@howtobooks.co.uk
www.howtobooks.co.uk

First edition 2005
Reprinted 2006

British Library Cataloguing in Publication Data
A catalogue record for this book is available from the British
Library

ISBN 13: 978 1 84528 048 2
ISBN 10: 1 84528 048 2

Edited by Francesca Mitchell
Cover design by Baseline Arts Ltd, Oxford
Produced for How To Books by Deer Park Productions,
Tavistock
Typeset by TW Typesetting, Plymouth, Devon
Printed and bound by Cromwell Press, Trowbridge, Wiltshire

NOTE: The material contained in this book is set out in good
faith for general guidance and no liability can be accepted for
loss or expense incurred as a result of relying in particular
circumstances on statements made in this book. The laws and
regulations are complex and liable to change, and readers should
check the current position with the relevant authorities before
making personal arrangements.

For Dominic and Max

Contents

Preface

This book is intended to meet a pressing need. Every day, large numbers of people contact executive search firms in the hope of finding a job or a non-executive directorship. Many of them do so without fully understanding the business of headhunting. We looked for a book to help such candidates, without success – and therefore decided to write one of our own.

This material has been developed from workshops that we have run (initially for graduates of INSEAD and the London Business School), on how to find your way through the executive search industry. The book is based on our experience with both executives and non-executive directors.

We have tested the manuscript on clients, candidates, colleagues and friends. In particular, we would like to thank the following for their ideas and feedback: Helen Barratt, Chris Bates, Gordon Cairns, Rashid Chinchanwala, Charles Cooper, Sara Cooper, Lucinda Daniel, Tom Daniel, Giles Daubeney, Caroline Deayton, *The Executive Grapevine,* Peter Greenslade, Anthony Harling, Michael Hartz, Laura Heybrook, Lydia Kan, Rupert Konstam, Francesca Lahiguera, David Lindsay, Steve Loffler, Andrew Lowenthal, Sarah McEwan, Julie Meyer, Sarah Morgan, Mark Mullen, Darryl

Noik, Jennifer Page, Anna Persin, Lord Poole, Margaret Purkiss, Renato Raho, Laura Renoldi, Alex Satchell, Sanjay Shah, Kerstin Shamma'a, Ranjan Singh, Mike Spurr, Andrei Stepanov and Susanne Worsfold. We are also very grateful to Michael Glover for his help with the chapter on non-executive directors.

John Purkiss
Barbara Edlmair
www.johnpurkiss.com

Introduction

Executive search has long been shrouded in mystique, and some of its practitioners try hard to keep it that way. Most people's knowledge of the sector is patchy, based largely on hearsay and the occasional unexpected phone call. However, executive search firms can provide access to some of the best career opportunities, so it is worth getting to know them. *How to Be Headhunted* will help you to do this, much more easily than before. It will open up a whole new world of opportunities.

Executive search is often referred to colloquially as 'head-hunting'. However, headhunting means different things to different people. Executive search is a much more clearly defined form of recruitment, in which a search firm charges a retainer to identify potential candidates through research and then to approach them directly. Many search firms restrict themselves to appointments with base salaries of £100,000 or more.

This book is above all intended for those who are actively looking for a new opportunity. Executive search firms are not necessarily the first place one would turn to, and with good reason. As a general rule, search firms like to take the initiative in approaching candidates.

If you *do* approach search firms yourself, you will need to understand the rules of engagement, which this book will help to clarify. Ideally, you should develop long-term relationships with search consultants throughout your career. However, many people do not get round to doing this while they are busy with their jobs. They only start contacting search firms when they have a specific need. Nevertheless, at any stage in your career there are things you can do to heighten your chances of being approached.

Of course, executive search is only *one* way to find your next role. In fact, you are much more likely to do so via your personal and professional network. However, if you establish and maintain contact with a number of search consultants, your network will be much more powerful, and will bring you more opportunities.

Finding your next job via a search firm has a number of advantages:

◆ You will have a much bigger network at your disposal.

◆ You will gain access to opportunities which you might not otherwise hear about.

◆ The search consultant can act as an intermediary between you and the employer. This includes giving you additional background information on the company and helping you to prepare for the interview. This is especially useful for obtaining feedback after interviews and during salary negotiations.

◆ The search firm effectively does most of the work for you, from setting up meetings to ensuring that you are given serious consideration as a candidate.

◆ You may have the opportunity to build a long-term relationship with the search firm. This will stand you in good stead throughout your career. A friendly search consultant can act as a useful sounding board on topics ranging from career development to remuneration packages.

It is, however, important to remember that search firms' clients are the *companies* wanting to recruit people. Unfortunately, search consultants are *not* paid to find *you* a new job. Nevertheless, if you know how executive search works, and understand consultants' needs, you can use this knowledge to your advantage. The better informed you are about executive search, the more a consultant will be able to help you.

This book will give you an overview of the executive search business and its processes, describing what search consultants are looking for, and why they might be interested in meeting you. It explains how to find the firms and the consultants most relevant to your needs, how to contact them and how to cultivate the relationship. It will also help you to define your unique selling proposition and to present it in a headhunter-friendly way. Finally, this book offers a few ideas to get you started if you are looking for an interim assignment or want to be a non-executive director.

In order to make *How to Be Headhunted* as relevant as possible, we have referred to specific firms with offices in the United Kingdom. While we have made every effort to check the facts prior to publication, there will have been some changes by the time you read this. However, the approach we recommend remains the same, and also applies to candidates living and working in other countries.

(1)

Who Are the
Headhunters?

HOW IT ALL BEGAN

Executive search emerged after the Second World War and rapidly established itself alongside other professional services. Search firms have divided and multiplied ever since, just like their peers in management consultancy, advertising and public relations. Although many headhunters are slow to admit it, most search firms trace their ancestry to a handful of pioneers. Most of these firms started in the USA and subsequently spread across the globe.

In 1946, Sidney Boyden, a consultant with Booz·Allen & Hamilton, founded what is now Boyden International. This is often considered to have been the first executive search firm. Heidrick & Struggles was founded in Chicago in 1953, by Gardner Heidrick and John Struggles. Spencer Stuart worked for them for a while and then founded his own firm in the same city in 1956. In 1964, Egon Zehnder left Spencer Stuart and founded Egon Zehnder International in Zürich. In 1969, Russell Reynolds founded Russell Reynolds Associates in New York. Lester Korn and Richard Ferry founded Korn/Ferry International in Los Angeles in the same year.

Heidrick & Struggles, Korn/Ferry, Spencer Stuart, Egon Zehnder and Russell Reynolds are the global giants which continue to spawn new firms at regular intervals. Some of them have decided to list on the stock market; Heidrick & Struggles and Korn/Ferry floated in 1999 on NASDAQ and the New York Stock Exchange respectively.

EXECUTIVE SEARCH IN THE UK

The UK is unusual in that one of the largest firms is descended from none of these five. Dr Anna Mann worked for a small search business before starting her own firm in 1976. Whitehead Mann gained a listing on the London Stock Exchange in 1997.

All the global search firms have offices in the UK – the second most mature and largest market after the United States. Executive search is a highly fragmented business, and the UK is no exception. According to *The Executive Grapevine*,[1] there are approximately 200 firms where the majority of the assignments involve base salaries of over £100,000. In the £40,000 to £100,000 category there is an even larger number. They range from one-man or one-woman bands to the large global firms, each employing over 100 staff in the UK.

The sector's vibrancy has also made it highly competitive in international markets. British firms frequently conduct pan-European and global assignments from the UK, and generate a significant portion of their revenues from clients based overseas.

---

[1] See www.executive-grapevine.co.uk

As in most markets, there is more than one route to success. The global firms obviously benefit from their ability to refer clients from one office to another. Provided they have staff with the right expertise, they can serve global clients in every part of their business. In recent years, some of the large firms have also used their relationships at board level to diversify into other areas such as executive coaching, talent retention programmes and management audit or appraisal.

Most of the smaller firms, sometimes referred to as 'boutiques', have maintained their focus on executive search. Many of the successful boutiques have been founded by consultants who were previously partners with a large international firm. Plenty of staff also move between search firms.

Sometimes smaller firms from different countries join together under one umbrella. This helps them to market their services and execute assignments internationally. Some are more closely connected than others, and they do not normally share a database. One example is the Amrop Hever Group, the world's largest independent organisation of owner-managed search firms.

CHANGING TIMES

During the internet boom which ended in 2000 the demand for candidates reached the point where the tables began to turn. *Candidates*, rather than clients, became the scarce resource. Some of them received calls from several search firms a day, and tended only to call back if they knew and respected the consultant, or at least the firm in question. It was suggested that headhunters had now become 'curators of talent'.

Executive search is highly cyclical; during the bear market which began in 2001, some search firms' revenues *halved*. The downturn was the worst for 20 years and, by 2003, a large number of executive search firms worldwide had gone out of business. The scales tipped back in favour of the clients, who were then able to obtain a better service on more favourable terms. Since the downturn, a number of new firms have sprung up, founded mostly by alumni of the larger ones.

TRACKING DOWN SEARCH FIRMS

The result of all this change is that the search consultants who are best placed to help you may be spread among the large and the small firms. This can be a challenge for candidates who drift out of touch with search firms while they focus on their jobs. When they re-emerge on the market, years later, they find that many consultants have moved on.

Another side-effect of the movement between firms is that most search consultants are in touch with former colleagues. Inevitably, they sometimes discuss candidates who have really made an impression on them, for better or worse! It is therefore best to do your homework, and approach each consultant with care. If you strike up a particularly good rapport, some consultants will introduce you not only to their colleagues but also to their counterparts in other firms.

The most comprehensive guide to search firms in the UK is *The Executive Grapevine*, updated annually and available in large reference libraries. Although this is an excellent publication, you should bear in mind that some firms, even small ones, present themselves as specialists in practically everything! Another useful source is *Executive Recruiters International*,[2] published by the US market research firm Hunt-Scanlon. We recommend that you take a book such as *The Executive Grapevine* as a starting point, and then ask people in your sector or function to recommend the firms and consultants that have impressed them most.

Search firms' websites also indicate their areas of specialisation, although the same caveat applies. It costs a firm nothing to say that they specialise in a particular area. In reality, they may not yet have completed any relevant assignments. Many of the bigger firms' websites will let you search for a consultant by location, by sector and sometimes by function. Some will also list their current assignments and let you register online. There is more information on how to find the right consultant in Chapter Three of this book.

Another starting point is the Association of Executive Search Consultants (AESC).[3] This is the trade association for retained executive search firms, i.e. those firms that charge a retainer, rather than being paid only when a candidate accepts a job offer. Its members promise to adhere to certain ethical standards.

By far the best way of finding a good firm or consultant continues to be by word of mouth. Ask your friends,

[2] See www.hunt-scanlon.com: Directories. *Executive Recruiters International.*
[3] See www.aesc.org

colleagues and peers if they have ever been in touch with firms which have impressed them, either as a candidate or a client. Even better, find out which firms are used by some of the companies you admire, and would really like to join.

Below is a selection of firms operating in the UK, to get you started. While it is by no means exhaustive, some of these names are likely to come up repeatedly as you do your research.

Please note that we have not included any one-man or one-woman bands, simply because there are too many of them for us to provide a meaningful list in the space available. Many are excellent in their field of specialisation. One way to track them down is by talking to other people who work in your sector or function.

A SELECTION OF EXECUTIVE SEARCH FIRMS OPERATING IN THE UK

Name	Comments	Web Address
Alexander Hughes	Offices throughout Europe	www.alexanderhughes.com
Armstrong International	Financial services	www.armstrongint.com
Axiom	Recruitment for the outsourcing sector	www.axiomexecutive.com
Barnes Kavelle	Based in Bradford	www.barneskavelle.co.uk

Black Appointments	Edinburgh and London	www.blackapp.co.uk
Blackwood Group	Strong in financial services	www.blackwoodgroup.com
The Bloomsbury Group	Financial and professional services	www.thebloomsburygroup.com
Boyden	Global firm	www.boyden.com
Cairns Bond	Based in Edinburgh	www.cairnsbond.com
Carbon	Strong in financial services	www.carbonleadership.com
The Curzon Partnership	Wide range of sectors	www.curzonp.co.uk
Egon Zehnder International	Large global firm	www.zehnder.com
EquityFD	Finance directors for growth businesses	www.equityfd.com
Fletcher Jones	Based in Edinburgh	www.fletcher-jones.co.uk
Fox Rodney Search	Legal	www.foxrodneysearch.com
Global Sage	Financial services	www.globalsage.com
Garner International	All sectors	www.garnerinternational.com
Gow & Partners	All sectors	www.gowpartners.com
Hanover Fox International	Several regional offices	www.hanoverfox.co.uk

Hanover Search & Selection	Financial services	www.hanover-search.com
Hanson Green	Well-known for non-executive directors	www.hansongreen.co.uk
Harvey Nash	Strong in information technology	www.harveynash.com
Heidrick & Struggles	Large global firm	www.heidrick.com
Highland Partners	Global firm	www.highlandsearch.com
Hogarth Davies Lloyd	Investment banking and legal	www.hogarthdavieslloyd.com
Hoggett Bowers	All sectors	www.hoggett-bowers.com
Holker Watkin	Permanent and interim	www.holkerwatkin.com
Howgate Sable	Several regional offices	www.howgate-sable.com
Imprint	All sectors	www.imprintplc.com
Ian Jones & Partners	All sectors except financial services	www.ianjonesandpartners.com
A.T. Kearney Executive Search	International firm	www.executivesearch.atkearney.com
KMC International	Mostly public sector	www.kmcinternational.co.uk
KPMG Executive Search and Selection	Best known for public sector work	www.kpmg.co.uk/searchandselection
Korn/Ferry International	Large global firm	www.kornferry.com

Lord Search and Selection	Based near Birmingham	www.lordsearch.co.uk
The Miles Partnership	All sectors	www.miles-partnership.com
Norman Broadbent	All sectors	www.normanbroadbent.com
Odgers Ray & Berndtson	UK operation of global firm	www.odgers.com
Oxygen Executive Search	All sectors	www.oxygenpeople.com
Penna	All sectors	www.e-penna.com
Purkiss & Company	All sectors	www.purkiss-company.com
Renoir Christian & Timbers	Technology	www.renoirct.com
The Rose Partnership	Financial services	www.rosepartnership.com
Russell Reynolds Associates	Large global firm	www.russellreynolds.com
Sainty, Hird & Partners	Financial services	www.saintyhird.com
Eric Salmon & Partners	Offices in Europe and New York	www.ericsalmon.com
Saxonbury	All sectors except financial services	www.saxonbury.com
Saxton Bampfylde Hever	Strong in public sector	www.saxbam.co.uk
Spencer Stuart	Large global firm	www.spencerstuart.com
33 St. James's	Search, selection and transition management	www.33stjamess.com

Tyzack Associates	Executive search and related services	www.tyzackassociates.co.uk
Veredus Executive Resourcing	Strong in public sector	www.veredus.co.uk
Walker Hamill	Strong in financial services	www.walkerhamill.com
Whitehead Mann Group	The UK's largest firm	www.wmann.com
Whitney Group	Financial services	www.whitneygroup.com
The Zygos Partnership	Board appointments	www.zygos.com

How Executive Search Works

WHERE DOES EXECUTIVE SEARCH FIT WITHIN RECRUITMENT?

Recruitment takes place in every sector, at all salary levels, and intermediaries are not always necessary. Many positions are filled by people the employer already knows, or via mutual contacts, press advertising or websites. It pays to be open-minded about how you will find your next job.

If an intermediary *is* involved, there are four approaches.

1. Executive search

2. Search and selection

3. Executive selection

4. Agencies

1. Executive search

This is a form of senior-level recruitment where a firm is retained by a client to find the right person for the job. Candidates are identified through research and then approached directly. Executive search assignments are almost always *exclusive*. In other words, a single firm is retained to do the work.

Executive search is used primarily for base salaries of £100,000 and above. The fee is typically a retainer divided into three monthly instalments, starting on day one of the assignment, and is paid regardless of the outcome of the search. There may then be a fourth invoice to reconcile the total fee to one third of the successful candidate's first-year remuneration.

Research typically involves three phases. In the first phase the researcher consults the firm's database, the internet, reference books, annual reports, subscription-based databases, trade publications and so on to identify suitable candidates. This is known as *desk research*. The second phase involves asking informed third parties, or *sources*, to recommend potential candidates or to provide more information about people the firm has already identified. In the third phase the search firm approaches candidates by telephone, perhaps accompanied by an explanatory letter or e-mail.

2. Search and selection
The figure of £100,000 is a crude dividing line between executive search, using only research, and *search and selection*, where research is combined with advertising. In other words, while the research is going on, the firm places an advertisement in one or more newspapers. The consultant selects the most promising responses, and interviews these candidates alongside those emerging from the research.

Search and selection is most widely used for assignments where the base salary is in the £40,000 to £100,000 range. As in executive search, the client usually pays a retainer in three instalments.

Some search consultants are reluctant to advertise, and appear wedded to using only research in all circumstances. However, there are jobs paying more than £100,000 for which a combination of research and advertising is highly effective. One example is senior roles within the finance function. Since practically all finance directors read the Financial Times, an advert in the recruitment section can be an effective means of attracting qualified candidates quickly.

Advertising can also be very helpful when the job is based in an unusual location. While it may prove difficult to convince most candidates to move, a minority of them will be positively attracted. An advertisement which clearly states where the job is based will naturally attract applications from people who want to work there.

Of course, there are sectors in which advertising is mandatory, particularly for the most senior roles. These include charities, government bodies, education, trade associations and the arts. They are collectively known as the 'not for profit' sector. For this sector, advertising helps to demonstrate that the recruitment process has been open and fair.

Some search firms also list their current assignments on their websites. Replying to an advertisement online is rather like responding to an advertisement in a newspaper.

3. Executive selection

Assignments for base salaries of £20,000 to £100,000 are sometimes handled purely by means of *executive selection*. The recruitment firm or the employing company places an advertisement in the newspaper or on an internet job board. They then select the best candidates from those who reply. Fees for this type of service tend to be lower, since no research is involved.

4. Agencies

Agencies tend to focus on candidates in the early stages of their careers. Candidates approach them when they are looking for a job, either because they know the firm's name already or because they have seen their advertisements on behalf of clients.

The agency sends candidates' CVs to companies which are looking for new staff. If a company wishes to employ someone, it pays a fee to the agency which presented the successful candidate. This type of recruitment is sometimes described as *contingent*, because the fee is dependent upon a successful outcome.

Agencies account for a large percentage of the market up to salaries of around £40,000. They are particularly active in areas where large numbers of people change jobs in the early stages of their careers, such as accountancy, law and IT.

HOW DOES EXECUTIVE SEARCH WORK?

Each search assignment is slightly different, depending on the client's requirements. However, there will normally be a number of basic steps, carried out to an agreed timetable:

- Briefing

- Research

- Long list

- Interviews with the consultant

- Short list

- Interviews with the client

- References and negotiations

- Formal offer of employment

- Acceptance of the offer.

One or more of these stages might be skipped if the client and the search consultant know each other very well, or if the client is under extreme time pressure. Some clients expect the search firm to cover the market thoroughly; others just want to meet a handful of qualified candidates quickly. The amount of paperwork involved can also vary greatly, depending on the search firm, the consultant and the client's preferences.

Before taking a closer look at the search process, it is time to introduce you to a key figure: the research associate.

BE NICE TO RESEARCH ASSOCIATES
For the sake of simplicity we have talked so far about *search consultants*, whose job involves winning new assignments, interviewing candidates, negotiating remuneration packages and taking references. Sometimes consultants also *approach* candidates, particularly if they already know them well.

However, in most cases it will be the *research associate* who contacts you.

Anyone who has had some contact with search firms will know that research associates play a crucial role. Thorough research is essential to produce a strong short list. In some firms the research team is a central function, working with each consultant as and when required. In other firms researchers are, like the consultants, members of a specialist practice.

Some researchers become consultants, while others decide to remain in research. This is often because they enjoy the work and the lifestyle suits their personal circumstances. Good research associates are well paid, and frequently develop specialist knowledge. Sometimes they take over quite a few of the consultant's responsibilities, although the consultant may be reluctant to admit this to clients.

In all likelihood it will be a research associate who discovers you, in one of the following ways:

◆ Finding your name during desk research

◆ Following up when someone else has recommended you

◆ Consulting the firm's database.

If you raise your profile you can increase your chances of being discovered in each of these three ways:

(a) Desk research
If you have published articles, spoken at conferences, been active in professional organisations or have given interviews

to the press, you are more likely to be identified through desk research. Before starting your job search, it is a good idea to make sure that this information is easily available, and that your name can be found on the internet using the most popular search engines.

It is also useful to check that your records in any alumni directories, online or offline, are up to date. Search firms frequently use them to track down candidates.

(b) Sources

Never underestimate the power of networking! If your job search is not confidential, you should tell your existing contacts that you are looking. Any one of them could receive a call from a search firm and then think of you.

It is best to check that your contacts have your correct phone number, together with your current or latest job title and the name of the company you work for. Most good research associates are very persistent, particularly if someone has recommended you enthusiastically. However, they are less likely to unearth you if they have been given a misspelt name to begin with. Anything you can do to make the research associate's life easier will improve your chances.

(c) Database

The firm's database is an important tool for researchers, and there are ways of ensuring that those who use it find you. You can read more about this in Chapter Five. In addition, research associates are likely to consult colleagues who have worked on similar assignments. The greater your visibility within the firm, the higher your chances of being considered for the latest assignment. We will discuss what you can do about this in Chapter Five also.

When you are approached as a *candidate*, you can actively help the researcher by returning calls promptly, providing clear information about yourself and having an updated CV ready. If you are not interested in the assignment, it is best to say so immediately rather than waste the researcher's time. If you are approached as a *source* for an assignment, we recommend that you listen carefully to the job description and try to come up with names of people you think might fit the brief. Avoid recommending your best mates over and over again, regardless of whether they are relevant. Researchers can spot this easily on the database, and it will not enhance your reputation. If you can give the correct spelling, title and contact details for the people you recommend, you will make yourself very popular indeed.

Although research associates meet fewer candidates than consultants do, they tend to speak to a lot more *potential* candidates on the telephone. This can give them an excellent sense of who might make a good candidate. You have to pass the research associate's screening process to make it to the next stage.

If you are known for helping researchers, there will be positive comments about you on the database. You will have established a relationship with the firm and may be one of the first to hear about an interesting new assignment.

In a large search firm there is also an information department, to which you may be asked to send your CV and covering letter in the first instance. This is usually because they receive such a quantity of 'write-ins' that someone spends part (or all) of each day putting them onto the database. If you fill in a registration form on the firm's website, your application is also likely to be handled by the information department in the first instance. You can find out more about how your CV is processed in Chapter Five.

WHAT HAPPENS DURING AN ASSIGNMENT?

The early stages

Clients often try to fill a vacant position through an internal promotion or by approaching someone they know in another company. If the right person cannot be found in either manner, they will then hire a search firm. In some cases the client uses a particular search consultant whom they know and trust. Otherwise, there may be a 'beauty parade' from which a search firm is chosen.

Ideally, an assignment should take no longer than three months. However, the average is longer than this, and the search firm will continue to look either until the position is filled or until the client cancels the assignment. Some particularly difficult searches have been known to drag on for one or two years!

Typically, the research associate plays a greater part in the early stages of an assignment, and the consultant in the later stages. Usually both attend a *briefing meeting* with the client. The aim is to learn more about the company's culture, define the job profile and gain a clear picture of the ideal candidate.

Meeting the client also gives them an initial 'feel' for the candidates who are likely to fit in terms of personal style.

After the briefing meeting the search firm drafts the *job specification*. This describes the company and the role, as well as the qualifications and experience required. It is effectively a selling document which will be sent out to candidates.

Becoming a candidate

The research phase usually lasts around six weeks. If your background seems appropriate, you will become a *candidate* for the assignment, even though you may not know about it. Some firms have a policy of collecting exhaustive background material and taking informal references before they approach a candidate; others will cold-call new contacts without hesitation. In either case, it helps if you are well-documented within the search firm. The more a researcher knows about you, the more likely they are to consider and approach you for an assignment which you will find interesting. If a search firm has your private contact details, it will also be easier for them to reach you confidentially.

The research associate is most likely to contact you by telephone. He or she may send an introductory e-mail or letter first, especially if you are hard to reach. Do not wait too long to return the call, and aim to speak during office hours; researchers have private lives too! When you speak to the researcher, listen carefully to find out if you are being approached as a candidate or as a source.

Acting as a source

If you are a *source*, the researcher will be hoping for insights into the industry, a particular company such as your previous employer, or the names of people you think are qualified. Do not worry whether they will be interested or not. It is the search firm's job to find that out. In some cases you may want your contact to know that you have recommended them; you can just ask the researcher to use your name. In other cases you can say you wish to remain anonymous. Good search firms always protect their sources.

Sometimes you may be approached as a source for an assignment which also interests *you*. This can be a delicate situation. Usually the researcher will know enough about you and the vacancy to sense whether there is a likely match. If you are being approached as a source rather than a candidate, there is usually a good reason for it. You may already be too senior for the job, or the remuneration package may be too low. Ask the researcher for more details. If the job still sounds perfect for you, by all means say you are interested.

If you do not mind the extra competition, you can be a source *and* a candidate. In other words, you can recommend people who could be suitable and register your own interest at the same time. The research associate will be grateful.

Finding out about the role

If you are approached as a candidate, listen carefully and ask brief questions to get a better idea of the role. Do not ramble on; the objective is to find out if there is mutual interest, without wasting anyone's time. If you are not well known to the search firm, you can give a brief overview of your current job and career to date. You are likely to be asked about your current role, the revenues for which you are responsible, the number of your direct reports, the title of the person you report to, the time you have spent in the role or the company, and your remuneration.

All of these questions help the researcher to work out if you are a relevant candidate. Even if you are not interested in this particular role, it is a good idea to answer the researcher's questions and to make sure that the search firm has your contact details. You can also send your CV to be added to the database. The firm may soon be handling another assignment which interests you more.

If you want to find out more about the role, the researcher will send you the job specification and expect you to send a CV. There will then be further telephone conversations to discuss the company, the job and your background, and to establish the potential 'fit'.

Confidential assignments

Occasionally, an assignment is confidential, and the researcher cannot disclose the client's identity. This sometimes arises because an executive is being replaced and has yet to be told. Alternatively, he or she may have decided to leave, but not everyone within the company may be aware of it. The search team will usually tell you as much about the role and the client as they can. However, it is not unusual to reach the interview stage of an assignment without knowing who the client is. You *may* be told if and when you make it to the short list. In the majority of cases you will be told the name of the company when you are first contacted over the telephone.

Reaching the long list

Once a researcher has established that you are qualified for an assignment, you may be added to the *long list*. This consists of everyone who appears qualified on paper, disregarding issues of 'style' and 'fit' for the time being. The length of the list depends on the assignment. There can be between five and fifty names – more in some cases.

The next step is usually for the search team to discuss the long list with their client, either face to face or over the phone. They should ask your permission before passing on any of your details to the client. The consultant may already have met some of the people on the long list, either during previous assignments or in connection with this search. Other candidates may only have been screened by the research associate over the phone. Sometimes the client will know some of the candidates already and eliminate them from the long list. In other cases, the brief description of their experience is enough for the client either to be very interested or to discount them altogether. The outcome of this discussion is a list of candidates whom the consultant agrees to interview.

If the search is confidential, the long list may take a slightly different form. Many firms apply the principle that candidates' identities should only be revealed to a client if the candidates already know the client's identity. If the client's identity is unknown, then the long list will refer to Candidate A, Candidate B, etc. The descriptions will be sparse enough to protect their identities.

Progress updates

Some time may have passed since you last heard from the search firm, and you may be wondering what is going on. Reputable firms do their best to keep candidates updated on the progress of an assignment. However, things can often drag on for longer than expected, especially when meetings need to be set up or when the client is travelling. No news is often good news. If you are no longer being considered as a candidate, you will normally be told swiftly.

After interviewing the candidates chosen from the long list, the consultant will put together a *short list*. This usually consists of between four and six people whom the client then interviews. In preparation for the client interviews, the consultant will write detailed *appraisals* describing each candidate's background and likely fit with the role in question. The preferred candidate generally emerges from this short list once the client has interviewed everyone.

Remuneration

The next stage is to negotiate the remuneration package. Money will not have been discussed in detail until now. Having checked your current salary early on, the researcher or consultant should only have continued talking to you if the remuneration made sense for you and your prospective employer. If you have been invited for an interview with the search firm, and remuneration has not been mentioned, it is usually assumed that an agreement can be reached.

The remuneration will now be discussed in more detail. For you as a candidate, the consultant can be a very useful intermediary at this point. They can help you to reach an agreement while preserving a friendly relationship with your new employer. The consultant will know the standard remuneration for the position and can help to keep emotions under control while an agreement is reached.

References

During the final stages of the assignment the search firm will take formal *references* on the preferred candidate. It is quite likely that *informal* references will have been taken earlier, perhaps even before you were contacted.

Some candidates have a ready supply of written references from their previous employers, which search consultants usually ignore. It is more likely that you will be asked to provide the names and phone numbers of former bosses, subordinates and peers whom the consultant can then call. He or she may also contact people you have not mentioned, to ask their point of view. If you have not yet resigned from your job, the consultant will not contact your current employer for a reference at this stage.

You can speed up the process by having a list of people ready who are qualified and willing to act as referees. It is important to contact them beforehand to refresh their memory of you and to make sure their contact details are up to date.

Reference-checking should be a two-way process; it is up to you to do your homework on the company. The search consultant will be able to offer some insights. It is also very helpful to speak to former employees, particularly those who may have reported to your prospective boss. You may be able to track down these people through your own network, or with the help of the search firm. A good firm will want you to join the company with your eyes open, so you are fully aware of the challenges as well as the opportunities.

The consultant will typically write a summary of the referees' comments to send to the client. Confidentiality is preserved by not attributing particular statements to individuals. This means that the document will start with a list of the names and job titles of the referees and their relationship to you. This will be followed by a summary of your referees' opinions regarding your personality, work style and achievements. In parallel, the search firm will usually check your qualifications with the relevant institutions.

If the references are unsatisfactory, or if the preferred candidate does not accept the offer, the client may decide to reconsider one of the remaining candidates on the short list. Once the final candidate has emerged, the consultant will let the remaining short-listed candidates know the outcome and pass on the client's feedback. After assignments are completed, consultants tend to stay in touch with their placed candidates at least until they have settled into new jobs, often for considerably longer. Consultants are not allowed to approach a placed candidate for another position while the candidate remains with the employer. However, there is often a continuing rapport between the placed candidate and the consultant. It is not unusual for placed candidates to become clients of the search firm that placed them.

3

Who Should You Approach?

In Chapter One we explained how to identify the search firms relevant to your background. The next step consists of finding those consultants within the firm who specialise in your area. At a senior level, the relationship with the right consultant is ultimately more important than the relationship with a particular search firm. It is worth taking time to identify consultants, as you will want to build a long-term relationship with *them*. If you target the wrong people, they will be unable to help you.

LOOK FOR CONSULTANTS WHO SPECIALISE IN YOUR AREA

As we mentioned earlier, the UK is the world's second largest executive search market, after the USA. As you might expect, most consultants in the UK specialise in either a sector or a job function. This gives them an edge in competing for a particular brief. They will have a 'feel' for the salary required to attract candidates, and an in-depth knowledge of relevant companies. Specialists are also more likely to have existing relationships with potentially suitable candidates. This helps to ensure that their phone calls will be returned when they are handling an assignment.

Clients often seek out consultants with specialised knowledge, whether they work in a large or a small firm. Most of the large search firms allocate their consultants to areas of specialisation, frequently known as 'practices'.

It is important for you as a candidate to identify the consultants most likely to include you on a short list. These are the people with whom you should aim to build long-term relationships. The best way to identify them is by word of mouth; they will tend to be well-known among people in your line of work. Alternatively, you can look at search firms' websites. They often provide information on areas of specialisation and the names and biographies of their consultants. *The Executive Grapevine* and *Executive Recruiters International* are also very useful for this purpose. If all else fails, you can simply call the firm's switchboard and ask if they have any consultants specialising in your field.

If you are still not sure which consultants are relevant to you, you can always send your CV and covering letter to the information departments of the larger firms. Their e-mail address is usually given on the firm's website. Once they have processed your CV, they will normally forward it to the relevant practice. If you are planning a radical career change, make sure that your target sector or preferred role is clearly stated in your covering letter.

Sectors

In the larger firms the practices are often subdivided. A typical classification is as follows:

Consumer	Communications/advertising
	Fast-moving consumer goods
	Hospitality and leisure
	Luxury goods
	Media
	Retail
Financial Services	Asset management/private banking
	Corporate finance
	Debt capital markets
	Equity capital markets
	Insurance
	Retail banking
Healthcare	Biotechnology
	Hospitals
	Medical devices
	Pharmaceuticals
Industry	Automotive
	Aviation
	Business-to-business/industrial services
	Chemicals
	Construction/property
	Energy
	Manufacturing
	Mining and metals
	Transport
Not for Profit	Arts
	Charities
	Education
	Government

	Non-governmental organisations
	Trade associations
Professional Services	Legal
	Management consultancy
	IT services
Technology	Electronics, including semiconductors
	Hardware
	Software
	Telecoms

In addition, some firms have teams serving the venture capital and private equity sectors. They focus their marketing efforts on the investors, and then recruit people for the companies in the investors' portfolios. These can range from start-ups to large management buy-outs.

Most consultants in the big firms are members of a practice, and often work with members in other countries. This also enables the practice to manage global client relationships, including 'off-limits' agreements, which we will discuss in Chapter Six. Specialisation has proved essential in areas such as financial services, where the large firms compete with boutiques focused on one or two niches.

Other types of specialisation

Some search firms, both large and small, have specialists in a particular *function* which is easily transferable across sectors. Finance, human resources, IT and strategy all lend themselves to this approach. The specialists get to know a particular candidate pool very well and then move from sector to sector, applying their knowledge to each company's particular needs. Very large firms can also have functional specialists within a practice, e.g. an IT specialist within financial services.

Some search consultants specialise by *level*, or seniority within the client organisation. However, this level usually turns out to be the board of directors, as defined in the UK to include both executive and non-executive directors. In other words, they recruit chief executives, non-executive directors, chairmen, and so on. Some large search firms have *board practices* which focus on this. These are also in effect functional practices, since they spend most of their time finding candidates with skills which can be transferred from one sector to another.

At one stage the most senior searches, particularly for chairmen and chief executives, tended to be carried out by partners in the large search firms. However, since 2000 there has been a great deal of fragmentation, with many partners leaving the large firms and setting up new ones. It is now just as likely that a small firm will handle a big search.

Some firms have practices specialising in a particular *region*, such as the Middle East or Central and Eastern Europe. These practices are often based in London.

In conclusion, for you as a candidate it is important to investigate both large and small search firms. What counts is the calibre of the search consultant, and their client base.

The last two chapters have given you an understanding of how executive search works. The next question is, what are search firms looking for?

$$\left(4 \right)$$

What Search Firms Are Looking for

Some people send off their CV to lots of search firms, with a covering letter or e-mail beginning 'Dear Sir/Madam'. This is not an approach we recommend.

It pays to understand what search firms are looking for. The first step is to take a close look at the firm's website. Do they recruit people with your type of background? Are you in the right salary range for their assignments?

Some firms post their current assignments on their website. If you fit one of the profiles, you are likely to be received with open arms. However, it is worth building a long-term relationship with the firm and its consultants in any event. They may or may not have an opportunity for you right now. Statistically speaking, they are *more* likely to have something for you later in your career.

When you market yourself to search firms, it is important to understand the needs of your 'customers' by looking at things from their point of view. Here are some factors to keep in mind.

SEARCH CONSULTANTS ARE PAID BY THE CLIENT

This is the most important thing to remember. Unless you happen to fit one of their current assignments, there is no pressing need for a search consultant to talk to you. Typically, consultants will be reluctant to read your CV, speak to you or meet you unless they can present you as a candidate for a current assignment. To put it bluntly, if search consultants spent all their time helping people with their job searches, they would not be in business for very long. There are exceptions to this however, and later in this chapter we will examine some of the reasons why a consultant might be interested in meeting you.

SEARCH CONSULTANTS ARE BUSY PEOPLE

Search consultants and research associates work on several projects at once, for different clients, often under great time pressure. They will appreciate it if you communicate clearly and efficiently. If your CV is difficult to read, then you are putting yourself at a disadvantage. It might end up in a 'to do' pile rather than being processed immediately. For this reason we will devote the whole of Chapter Eight to preparing a 'headhunter-friendly' CV.

SEARCH CONSULTANTS NEED CONFIDENTIAL INFORMATION

Once you are confident that you are dealing with a reputable search firm, it is best to share information with them freely. You can expect the search firm to treat your information in confidence. There are certainly examples of less reputable firms forwarding CVs to clients without the candidates' permission. However, a firm which wants to preserve and enhance its standing will never do this. The best way to be absolutely sure is to ask other people about the firm's reputation. If someone has had a bad experience they are very likely to tell you! You can also emphasise to the consultant that you are talking to them in confidence.

This is as much as you can do. If you are any more cautious, you risk irritating the consultant or researcher. They need confidential information in order to help you, and to do their job.

You should certainly tell the search firm your current remuneration package. Some candidates worry that they will be regarded as too expensive, particularly if there are lots of other people looking for jobs. However, the firm should know what the market rates are. If you want to avoid missing out on an opportunity, you can emphasise that you are flexible about what you earn in your next role.

SEARCH CONSULTANTS NEED YOU TO BE HONEST

It is amazing that some very senior people think they can lie on their CVs, or in an interview, and get away with it. However, good search firms take lots of references on candidates and check qualifications with the universities and professional bodies in question. If someone has deliberately misled them, the firm is unlikely to contact them ever again. Given what we said in Chapter One about the personal contacts between search firms, it is likely that the bad news will travel fast.

The majority of candidates *are* honest, but some of them are less open than they could be. Imagine that you fell out with your boss in one of your previous jobs. It is best not to say this on your CV. Instead, you can write something like, 'I resigned and looked for a new opportunity'. This begs the question 'why?', which the consultant is likely to raise during your interview. As long as you couch your answer in balanced, rational terms, then you will be taken seriously. The important point is that *you* told the search firm first, rather than leaving them to stumble on this information later.

REASONS WHY A SEARCH CONSULTANT WOULD MEET YOU

We have looked at what search firms expect from candidates in terms of behaviour and disclosure. Now, why should they meet you, and what specifically are they looking for?

There are five main reasons why a consultant might want to meet you:

(a) You are a relevant candidate for a current assignment

Your background may be appropriate for one of the search firm's current assignments. In this case they will be very pleased to hear from you, since your arrival will help them to assemble a strong short list quickly.

Even if you encounter strong interest initially, it is worth finding out exactly what the search firm is looking for. There are plenty of candidates who seem right at first, but who subsequently rule themselves out because the consultant begins to feel that they would not fit well with the client.

(b) You are a potential short-list candidate

In Chapter Three we talked about the way consultants and research associates specialise in order to gain a competitive advantage. If they have conducted many searches in the same market, then they may know at the outset several candidates who will end up on the short list. Although there are many executives to choose from, only a limited number are excellent in a particular field.

If your background looks promising, the consultant may want to meet you as a potential short-list candidate for a future assignment. This will enable them to complete new searches more quickly and efficiently. The more specialised the consultant in your particular area, the more likely this is to occur. When they meet you on a general basis, consultants will probably spend less time with you than if you were a candidate for an existing assignment. However, it is still useful to have met face to face.

You may even be able to help the consultant to win an assignment. As we mentioned earlier, consultants should never disclose your identity to a potential client without your permission. However, they *can* say that they know a candidate who has relevant experience, and is looking for a new opportunity.

You can also agree to be a benchmark candidate. As we mentioned earlier, research can take up to six weeks. In some cases this is necessary, particularly for an international assignment. However, if the client briefs the search firm, and several weeks elapse before they discuss the long list, there is always a risk that the search team will go up a blind alley. One way the consultant can avoid this is to present a benchmark candidate very early on in the assignment. This helps the consultant to discover quickly whether the search is on target. If not, then the client's feedback enables them to adjust swiftly and save a great deal of time.

Some candidates are wary of being the benchmark, preferring to go last. However, in our experience, the benchmark candidate is *at least* as likely to be offered the job as the other short-list candidates. If the search consultant's hunch is accurate, then the first candidate has a better than average chance.

By agreeing to be a benchmark candidate, you are helping the consultant to build a stronger relationship with their client, and complete the assignment. They will be grateful to you for this. Another advantage is that they will write a full appraisal on you. As we will see in the next chapter, this is a step forward in raising the search firm's awareness of you – increasing the likelihood that you will be short-listed for other assignments.

(c) You are a potential client

Another reason why a search consultant meets people is to identify potential clients. Consultants are always on the look-out for new clients and assignments, and the competition is often fierce. They might be willing to meet you just to get to know you, so they have an advantage if you ever hire a search firm yourself.

As a candidate, it is best to approach this topic with care. To begin with, it pays to be realistic about whether you could become a client of the search firm in question. You can gauge this by considering the people who report to you, or are likely to do so in your next job. Are their salaries high enough to fit the criteria of the search firm in question? If you are an HR director, are you likely to commission assignments which would be of interest to this firm?

You can often work out the answers by looking at the firm's literature or website, or by asking one or two questions. If you suggest you could become a client when you are not yet senior enough, then the search consultant may conclude that you have not done your homework, or lack judgement, or both.

By avoiding inappropriate assumptions about your potential value as a client, you can keep your options open. Even if you know that you could be a client one day, there are good reasons for keeping quiet about it. You can then watch and listen carefully.

Senior executives report an amazing range of experiences when they approach search firms as candidates. Some consultants go out of their way to be helpful, regardless of whether there is a direct benefit to them in the short term. This includes introducing strong candidates to other search consultants in the same field who are, in principle, competitors. A friend of ours in another firm calls this 'karmic executive search'. You do as much good as you can, to as many people as possible – and at some point, good things will come back to you, from the most unexpected sources.

At the other extreme are consultants who do not return candidates' phone calls or reply to their letters or e-mails. Others are critical or dismissive if they do eventually meet them. They give the impression that they are doing candidates an enormous favour by seeing them in the first place.

Most search consultants are somewhere between these two extremes. If you observe carefully, it will become very clear which consultants handle candidates in the most professional manner. You can then decide whom to use for *your* assignments in future.

(d) You have been recommended by someone who is important to the consultant

Search firms want to stay on excellent terms with existing or potential clients, as well as influential groups whose members could also be clients at some point. If you contact a consultant on the recommendation of someone who is important to them and their business, they may meet you for the sake of the other person. Equally, if you are a graduate of the same business school, or belong to the same organisation, then the consultant is more likely to meet you or have a discussion over the telephone.

Probably the best introduction to a search firm is a letter or phone call from someone they respect, recommending you personally. If this third party is an existing or potential client, then one of their consultants is very likely to meet you. The next best thing is a letter from you, mentioning the person whom you and the consultant both know. You will find an example in Chapter Nine.

(e) The consultant wants information on your colleagues

There is a fifth potential reason why search consultants may decide to meet you. This is to gather information on your current employer and your colleagues. It is fine to make general comments about people you both know, or confirm who does which job in your organisation. Most consultants want to be up to date and are inveterate name-droppers; it boosts their credibility with clients and candidates. If at any stage you feel uncomfortable answering the consultant's questions, it is best to say so.

To sum up, there are many reasons why a search consultant may decide to meet you; it is often best to find out their particular needs when you meet. You can then tailor your approach accordingly.

Having read this chapter you are able to think through the needs of the market you are about to approach. The next chapters are about building awareness and overcoming obstacles.

$$\left(5 \right)$$

Building Awareness

Some people assume that word of their talents will spread, and headhunters will then start calling them. At the other extreme are candidates who believe that search firms need constant reminders, including frequent phone calls and e-mails attaching the same CV again and again!

The reality is somewhere in between. There *are* things you can do to become better known. Consultants and researchers will then think of you when the right opportunity comes up. On the other hand, it is best to do this with a light touch, to avoid being regarded as a nuisance.

HIERARCHY OF AWARENESS

As in any other market, those who might need your services have a patchy knowledge of what is on offer. For each consultant or research associate, there is effectively a *hierarchy of awareness*, shown on the opposite page.

We will discuss these levels of awareness from the bottom up.

(a) You are invisible

This is the first extreme, mentioned above. If you do nothing, you may rarely, if ever, receive phone calls from search firms.

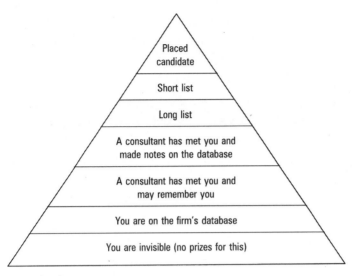

Hierarchy of awareness

Of course, a search firm could come across you during an assignment. If you are very good at your job, then former colleagues, or even the people you work with now, may recommend you. If you are active in trade associations or other industry bodies, you will become more visible. If you have spoken regularly at conferences, or are an acknowledged media pundit, then research associates may track you down. However, there is no guarantee of this, and a direct approach to search firms is definitely worthwhile.

You can greatly improve your chances of being approached by sending your CV to a number of search firms, in the right manner. Some firms also allow you to fill in a registration form over the internet. In either case, your aim is to be included on the company's database. Do not expect to hear back from them unless you happen to fit a current assignment. Some firms may send you an e-mail or a letter as an acknowledgement; most will not. It is best *not* to follow up with a phone call. If the firm has a relevant assignment, one of its researchers or consultants will contact you.

Making it onto the firm's database is already an achievement, and you will only get there if you have targeted the right firm in the first place. Having read this far, you know how to identify the appropriate firms and consultants. Their websites will also give you strong clues about whether your background is likely to be of interest. A website will usually tell you the sectors in which they work, and sometimes the salary ranges too. If you send your CV to a firm which does not work in your field or at your level, they will sometimes tell you they cannot help you. More often, you will hear nothing from them, and your CV will head straight for the shredder.

Even if your background *is* highly relevant and you are a potential candidate for an assignment, you can improve your chances further. One of the best ways is to make life easier for the person receiving your CV. This includes writing it in the 'headhunter-friendly' format we recommend in Chapter Eight.

It is also a good idea to send your CV in electronic form so that it can be attached to the firm's database. This enables everyone in the firm to retrieve it when required. In theory, if your paper CV is really interesting, someone might decide to scan it. However, since current assignments always take precedence, your precious document may end up in the 'pending' tray of an overworked secretary. A clear e-mail with your CV attached is the best means of ensuring that the firm includes you on its database right away.

(b) You are on the firm's database

Once you are on the database, everyone in the firm can retrieve your details when required. This is a good start. However, a large firm's database may include over a million people worldwide, so you should not hold your breath!

Your work experience will normally be coded by industry and by job function, so that consultants and research associates can find you quickly. Search firms tend to use SIC (Standard Industrial Classification) or similar codes to describe the sectors in which you have worked. They then use function codes to describe your jobs with each company. This enables research associates to retrieve the records of all candidates who meet the criteria for a particular assignment.

It is vitally important that you are coded correctly, so your name comes up in relation to the appropriate sector and job function. You can help to ensure this happens by making your CV as clear as possible. Particularly if you have worked for a small company which is not well known, you should include a brief description of what it does. You should also explain your responsibilities as clearly as possible.

Once you have sent your CV to a number of search firms, we recommend that you stay in touch with the five to ten firms you believe are most relevant to your career. When you move jobs or are promoted, let these firms know and make sure they have your updated CV.

You can also act as a helpful source of information, responding promptly to researchers' phone calls and recommending potential candidates. Even if no one from the firm has ever met you, they are likely to make positive comments about you on the database. You may then be classified as a 'helpful source'. This increases the likelihood that you will hear about opportunities which could interest you. As soon as the search firm wins an assignment for which your background is directly relevant, the consultant or research associate will call you.

While you are talking to staff at the search firm, you can check in passing that your current CV is attached to their database and that you have been coded correctly. Incidentally, under the Data Protection Act you have a right to know what information the firm holds on your file. You can also ask to be taken off a firm's database at any time.

(c) A consultant has met you and may remember you

This is better than just being on the database, but not necessarily by much! Keyboard skills vary greatly from one consultant to another, and some do not always switch on their computers. Notes may or may not end up on the database, where colleagues can read and use them. Some consultants still subscribe to the view that 'knowledge is power'. They keep as much information as possible in their heads, or in their own cardboard folders.

Of course, many consultants and research associates are very diligent. Some firms make the quality of database entries a factor in qualifying for bonuses. However, there are alarming stories about Consultant A meeting Mr Outstanding and neither telling Consultant B nor making any meaningful entries on the database. Consultant B then wins and completes an assignment, without considering Mr Outstanding, even though he would have been an excellent candidate!

There is not much you can do about this, other than to check that you are on the database and correctly coded. A research associate, a consultant's personal assistant, or someone in the information department is probably best placed to help you.

(d) A consultant has met you and made notes on the database

This is a big improvement on (c) above. Since databases usually function across all the firm's offices, everyone can now read about you and consider you for relevant assignments. The consultant's comments will bring your database entry to life and will be much more persuasive than your CV on its own.

(e) You have been on a long list

The long list consists of all the candidates the search team has identified as relevant to a particular assignment. Sometimes this list exists only in virtual form: relevant candidate records are linked to the assignment on the firm's database. The list can then be printed out whenever required, for internal discussion. In other cases the long list may be a working document in printed form which is updated at regular intervals.

Whatever the format, being on the long list is a step forward in the firm's awareness of you. There will normally be comments by the consultant or research associate, discussing your suitability as a candidate.

Whether or not you make it onto the short list for this assignment, you are starting to become known within the firm. Researchers and consultants working on similar assignments in the future will usually take a close look at the long list. It will help them identify their first few relevant candidates, and you could be among them.

Please note that you may be included on a long list without meeting the search consultant. This can occur if you have a strong CV and have been recommended by several people. However, the search firm should only forward information about you to the client with your permission. If the client is interested to find out more, the consultant will then meet you for an interview.

(f) A consultant has presented you as a short-list candidate
By this stage the consultant will have met you and written a detailed appraisal on you, describing your experience and assessing your suitability for the role in question. These appraisals are usually kept as an attachment to the database.

When the next assignment comes up, you are already well documented. You are more likely to be added to the long list and perhaps the short list. During a discussion of the long list, a client will frequently ask the consultant if they have met any of the candidates mentioned. If the same consultant is handling this new assignment, it makes a good impression if they are able to describe you vividly. If you have been on a short list before, you are also ideally placed to be a benchmark candidate, as discussed in Chapter Four.

It is quite common for short list candidates to become clients of the firm, even if they do not get this particular job. If the search team has handled them professionally, candidates may feel that this would be a good firm to represent their own companies. Many clients are quite rightly concerned that all candidates are treated well, since it enhances their company's reputation among an influential group of people.

(g) Placed candidate

Congratulations!

6

Common Obstacles

So far we have focused on how you can build and maintain awareness of what you have to offer. However, there may be other factors which determine whether you are considered for an assignment. Some of them are nothing to do with you personally, but can block your path nonetheless. Two of the most common issues are *parallel processing* and *off-limits agreements*.

PARALLEL PROCESSING

Parallel processing is where a search firm allows you to be on the long list or short list for two or more clients at once. Some firms are strictly against this practice, believing you should only be a candidate for *one* of their assignments at a time. This means that, so long as you are 'reserved' for assignment A, you cannot be approached for assignment B. This applies even if the two assignments are being handled by two consultants in different offices.

Even in firms which do not allow parallel processing there is often keen competition for the best candidates. While you are on the short list for assignment A, you may still be considered unofficially for assignment B, even though nobody has contacted you for B yet. The researcher for assignment B will pester the researcher for A until you are either hired by client A or are 'released' for B. All this can go on without your knowing about it. You may be licking your wounds after being turned down by company A. Moments later the phone rings and the same search firm starts talking to you about assignment B!

What should you do to maximise your chances of being considered for a variety of assignments? Unfortunately, there is not much you can do, except to withdraw swiftly from assignments which do not really interest you. You can also introduce yourself to a number of search firms, to increase the number of assignments for which you are considered. You may be pleased to hear that parallel processing is more common these days.

OFF-LIMITS AGREEMENTS

Off-limits agreements can greatly affect the number and quality of approaches you receive. There are two kinds of off-limits agreement: (a) those relating to a person such as a placed candidate, and (b) those relating to a company or part of a company.

The majority of reputable search firms have a rule that placed candidates should never be approached for a new assignment, for as long as they remain with their current employer. There is frequently an off-limits agreement with the client which underlines this point. However, as soon as you move to Company B, the search firm which placed you at Company A will be able to approach you again. Relationships between search consultants and executives can last for many years. In some cases a consultant may place a candidate several times, quite legitimately.

Off-limits agreements can also affect the people working with that placed candidate, or working in an area of the client's business which has recently employed a search firm. Whenever a search firm handles an assignment for a client, there is a potential conflict of interest. The firm must get to know at least *some* of the client's employees, to ensure that the candidates they present are a good fit. However, this knowledge could also be useful in placing those employees elsewhere!

The off-limits agreement is intended to remove this conflict of interest. At the most basic level, the search firm agrees not to approach the placed candidate's immediate colleagues for at least a year. There are also more complex agreements, whereby a subsidiary, a division or even the whole company is declared off-limits to the search firm. In return, the client may guarantee the firm a minimum volume of business.

Non-executive directors are not usually subject to off-limits constraints. The search firm can place the same candidate with several different clients.

If a search firm enters into too many off-limits agreements there will be very few organisations where it can approach candidates. The bigger the firm, the more this has to be kept under control. The firm's consultants may also identify certain *academy companies* for which they *will not* work. These companies are then treated purely as sources of candidates.

Some clients distribute their assignments among several firms, with the aim of putting their staff off-limits to as many as possible. Search firms are wise to this, and there can be lively negotiations of 'off-limits' in return for agreed volumes of business. There is even a story about a consultant who called a particular client once a year to ask for new assignments. This was on the understanding that he would put the company off-limits for another 12 months!

What does this mean for you? Quite simply, if your employer has recently used a particular search firm, you may be off-limits. No matter how relevant your background and how well-written your CV, the firm cannot consider you for an assignment. It is worth checking this, particularly when dealing with large search firms. A research associate or someone in the information department is usually the best person to call. You can say you are considering sending in your CV, and want to check first whether you are off-limits.

If you are already on the database, the organisation which employs you will be shown as either 'off-limits' or 'open'. If you are *not* on the database, the person you speak to will normally be able to check whether your company or your division is off-limits. They can simply enter the name of your employer and read the notes describing any agreement there may be.

If you discover you *are* off-limits, there are two possible courses of action. One is to do nothing. This is recommended if you do not want your employer to know that you are looking for a new job. However, they may already have announced their intention to let you go, or you may have told them you want to move on. Under these circumstances, they may 'release' you from the off-limits agreement, by sending a letter to the search firm.

In this chapter we have discussed how to overcome obstacles where possible. Our next three chapters are about marketing yourself to executive search firms. This involves defining your unique selling proposition and preparing your CV and covering letter.

7

Your Unique Selling Proposition

When approaching executive search firms, it is useful to have a list of characteristics that make you different from other candidates. By thinking carefully about your qualifications, skills and experience, you can distil them into five or six points.

One good reason for doing this is that search firms tend to use five or six criteria to select candidates. If you can adapt your approach to *their* way of thinking, you will make their job easier – and you are also more likely to be considered.

THE ACID TEST

This term describes the five or six criteria used by search firms to evaluate candidates for a particular assignment. The criteria should be objective and measurable.

Here is an example of an Acid Test:

◆ Qualified accountant or MBA

◆ A successful track record managing a business with revenues of at least £20m

◆ A minimum of five years' experience in semiconductors

◆ Experience of acquisitions and divestments

◆ Good spoken French

Some consultants take this a step further by applying a methodology known as 'competency-based' interviewing. Like many useful techniques, this is sometimes shrouded in jargon. Essentially, the assessment is based on what you have *done*, rather than what you *say* about yourself. The consultant asks a series of probing questions about what you did in particular situations during your career to date. They then draw conclusions about how you would perform in the job under discussion.

You will notice that all the criteria listed in the example above are measurable, to a greater or lesser degree. At the same time, the search team will take into account a range of other 'soft' skills, such as the ability to lead and influence people, adapt to different corporate and national cultures, etc. However, the 'hard' criteria listed in the Acid Test are the first filter through which candidates must pass in order to be included on the long list.

Before we turn to your *unique selling proposition*, we would like to highlight a common pitfall.

AVOID LABELLING YOURSELF
The best way to approach search firms is to supply them with relevant *facts* about yourself. Instead, many candidates make the mistake of providing *opinions* about their personalities and character traits instead. They do this in 'pen

portraits' on their CVs, in their covering letters, and even during the interview. Here are some favourites:

'I am very hands-on.'
'I am entrepreneurial.'
'I am a team-player.'

or even:

'I am an entrepreneurial, hands-on team-player.' (An EHOT?)

There are several difficulties with this approach. The first is that consultants and researchers are trying to gather objective information to determine whether you are a relevant candidate. If you start writing this sort of thing on the front page of your CV, you will have no room for more important facts. A consultant's time is limited so it is best to get straight to the point.

Secondly, describing yourself in this way will not strengthen your position; quite the reverse in fact. Most search consultants feel it is *their* job to form a view on what you have to offer. Putting it bluntly, they do not want to be spoon-fed your opinions about yourself! They may even conclude that you are unfamiliar with executive search, which will not help their perception of you.

The third difficulty is that these statements are vague, referring to things which are very difficult to measure. Therefore, they do not contribute to the selection process, and most search consultants will ignore them.

Claims that you are 'hands-on' or a 'team-player' are practically useless to someone trying to decide whether you are a relevant candidate. Imagine if we gathered together all the candidates currently looking for a job, and asked them if they possessed these attributes. Most would say yes to both of them! If you write in clichés, you also risk being seen as someone who lacks originality.

The word 'entrepreneurial' is widely misused. Some people refer to themselves as 'entrepreneurial' when they really mean 'energetic' or 'dynamic'. There are similar difficulties with describing yourself as a 'leader'. Some candidates feel that they have particularly good interpersonal skills, and that this differentiates them from other people. The difficulty is that almost no candidate would say they had *bad* interpersonal skills!

It is best to stick to measurable facts when describing yourself. If you have a talent for getting on with people, this should become clear during the interview. The best way of getting your point across is to describe a real situation where you have demonstrated these qualities.

DEFINING YOUR UNIQUE SELLING PROPOSITION

Now that we have pointed out the pitfalls to be avoided, we can start work on your *unique selling proposition* (USP). The aim is to distil your key attributes into five or six bullet points which, when combined, make you unique. The more closely your USP matches the Acid Test for a particular assignment, the more likely you are to appear on the long list and then the short list.

The simplest bullet points are based on the qualifications you have which most other people do not. For example:

◆ MBA, London Business School

or:

◆ Chartered Accountant, first-time passes.

Even if you are one of over 200,000 qualified accountants in the UK, you can still be unique! The key to this is the other four or five bullet points.

If you have started a new business, it is best to include a bullet point which describes what happened. For example:

◆ Co-founded a software company which achieved annual revenues of £5m prior to a trade sale to XYZ Corporation.

This is much more powerful than saying vaguely, 'I am entrepreneurial'. If the consultant is looking for someone to join a start-up company, you will leap off the page!

It is quite likely that one of your bullet points will relate to the *stage* in a business' life where you have a particularly strong background. Besides start-ups, you could be experienced in turnarounds, management buy-outs, international expansion or winding up a company.

If you have experience of leading a team, it is best to describe this clearly. For example:

◆ Led a team of twenty drawn from eight European countries.

One might object that the USP ends up looking rather like the pen portraits which we recommend that you avoid. The differences are as follows:

1. The points in your USP are factual and measurable.

2. There should be no more than six of them.

3. Combined, they should differentiate you from most other candidates.

4. They should be in your covering letter rather than your CV.

Many people find it difficult to formulate a convincing USP on their own. Some of the books on CV-writing offer useful tips. It is also worth remembering that results can often be improved with outside help. During our workshops we usually sit people down in pairs, so that they can work on their USPs together. While one person describes their suggested USP, point by point, the other listens sympathetically, but critically. The latter's feedback helps to ensure that each point is clear, measurable and credible. When you are formulating your own USP, you may wish to do the same with a friend or family member.

FROM CV TO USP: A PRACTICAL EXAMPLE

Here is the first page of an invented CV, in the 'headhunter-friendly' format which we will be discussing in the next chapter.

SUNITA SHAH
Flat 3, 30 Hill Street, London W1 8VY, UK
Mobile: +44(0)7800 000000. Email: sunita@shah.com

PERSONAL DETAILS

Date of Birth: 10th October 1972
Nationality: British and Indian

CAREER TO DATE

2002–2005   ONLINE TRAVEL PLC
Head of Southern Europe, based in Milan
(revenues: £50m)

1998–2002   EXTRATERRESTRIAL SOFTWARE, INC
(an IT services business with revenues of £60m)

2000–2002   Business Manager, Europe (revenues: £30m)
1998–2000   Business Development Manager, eBusiness

1993–1997   VEDASOFT, INC

1995–1997   Business Development Manager
1993–1995   Marketing Executive, Delhi

EDUCATION
1998   INSEAD
MBA

1990–1993   LONDON SCHOOL OF ECONOMICS
BSc Economics (2.1)

LANGUAGES

English: Mother tongue
Hindi: Fluent
French: Fluent
Italian: Working knowledge

Based on the one-page CV shown above, here is a suggested USP for Sunita Shah:

◆ Experience as general manager of a £50m online travel business.

◆ Eight years' experience in software: in marketing, sales and general management.

◆ International experience in Europe and India.

◆ Multilingual: English, French, Italian and Hindi.

◆ INSEAD MBA.

These five points are factual and concise. In combination they make this candidate almost certainly unique.

Your unique selling proposition will differentiate you from practically every other candidate and is particularly useful for covering letters, interviews and telephone conversations with search firms. If you are clear about what you have to offer, and what makes you different, you will be much more successful in marketing yourself.

8

Your CV

This chapter describes what we believe your CV should contain, and how it should be laid out. Your CV is critical to your success in approaching search firms. In most cases, the consultant will decide whether to meet you on the basis of this document and your covering letter, discussed in the next chapter.

It helps to think about your target market, and imagine your CV *at the point of use*. Research associates and members of the information department are most likely to read your CV in the first instance. They are extremely busy. If you are not directly relevant to a current assignment, they are likely to look at it for 20 to 30 seconds.

If your CV is well-written and well-structured, the reader can decide quickly what to do with it. If your CV is poorly presented, and the essential information is hard to find, then it may spend days or weeks in a 'pending' tray.

Many CVs are poorly written. They often contain grammatical errors and spelling mistakes. We will return to this subject in Chapter Ten. In the meantime we will show you our recommended format, to help you gain a favourable response.

A 'HEADHUNTER-FRIENDLY' CV

What we are describing here is a 'headhunter-friendly' CV. This is different from the format preferred by many managers in large companies, who often ask for no more than two pages. There are two reasons for the difference in approach. Firstly, search firms tend to receive far more CVs than employers do. Secondly, managers generally do not write appraisals, whereas search consultants usually do so for all the candidates they present to their clients. Search firms therefore tend to want a lot more information from your CV, and they want it to be both concise and detailed!

Here is how to give them both. For most search firms, an effective CV consists of two sections: (a) a one-page summary, and (b) a more detailed description, in two to three pages, of your career to date.

(a) The one-page summary

Many candidates send a two- to four-page CV which explains everything step by step. Their education and training are frequently relegated to the last page. Their early career is somewhere in the middle. If you do this, and yours is one of several hundred CVs matching the criteria, you have put yourself at a disadvantage.

It is always possible that the reader will discount you anyway, because your background is not relevant to a current assignment. In this case there is little you can do about it. However, if your background *is* relevant, you will want to make absolutely sure that they turn the page, read the rest of your CV, and put you on the long list. This is the point of the one-page summary.

A one-page summary grabs the reader's attention within seconds. Imagine the researcher or consultant working their way through 500 paper CVs, or clicking on CVs attached to a database. If you are relevant to a current assignment, this front page will be much appreciated. It will help to ensure that your CV goes onto the 'yes' pile, for further consideration, rather than the 'nos' or the 'maybes'.

The one-page summary consists of your personal details, education, training and career to date. This document should be easy to read and process *without* a covering letter or any supporting information. On the following page is a model for a one-page CV.

DAVID BROWN

Date of birth: 30/4/62
Married, with two children
72 Leicester Road, Birmingham
B3 5NH, UK

Home: +44 121 7000 0000
Work: +44 121 7111 1111
Mobile: +44 7770 123 123
david@brown.net

CAREER TO DATE

1999–Present   **THE MID-CAP COMPANY PLC**
Group Finance Director (revenues: £330m)

1994–1999   **THE MULTINATIONAL COMPANY, INC**

1996–1999   Finance Director, Cat Food Division (£300m)
1994–1996   Financial Controller, Dog Food Division (£280m)

1987–1994   **THE VERY BIG COMPANY PLC**

1991–1994   Manager, Financial Planning & Analysis
1987–1991   Financial Analyst

1983–1987   **THE BIG ACCOUNTANCY FIRM**
Audit Trainee to Audit Manager

OTHER

2000–Present   Non-Executive Director of Hi-Tech Software Plc

QUALIFICATIONS

1986   **INSTITUTE OF CHARTERED ACCOUNTANTS**
First-time passes. (Fellow 1996).

1983   **MANCHESTER UNIVERSITY**
BSc Economics, 2.1

LANGUAGES   English: mother tongue
French: fluent business level

Please note:

◆ The CV includes your name, telephone numbers and e-mail address. Your covering letter can easily become detached from your CV. In this case the search firm will still be able to contact you.

◆ Include as many phone numbers as you feel comfortable giving out. The easier you are to contact, the better. Daytime and mobile phone numbers are particularly helpful. If you include your work telephone number or e-mail, the search team will assume it is safe to use them.

◆ The e-mail address should be in *black*, not blue or any other colour which your word-processing software may suggest. Some laser printers print blue as white. In this case your e-mail address will magically disappear! The same can be true of any colours you may use for headings or text. We have received CVs which come out of the printer with no headings, as well as CVs in a fashionable shade of grey which come out completely white.

◆ Unless you are American, we recommend that you include your date of birth and age. This saves the search firm the extra work of estimating how old you are. If you *are* American, the search firm will probably avoid enquiring about your age if they are presenting you to a US client. However, they can still estimate it when they check your academic and professional qualifications with the relevant institutions.

◆ This one-page summary should only describe your employment history in outline: the name of the company, an indication of its size, and your title. If the company is not well-known, you should include a phrase or sentence to explain what it does. Further details can be postponed until the second section of the CV.

◆ Your education and training, including the dates, should all be on the front page. Some candidates put this on page 3, 4 or 5 of their CV. However, the busy researcher or consultant may never get that far!

Things to avoid

◆ Using the heading 'Curriculum Vitae'. It is already obvious and uses up valuable space in a prominent part of your CV.

◆ Beginning your CV with a 'pen portrait' or bullet-point description of yourself. These take up valuable space on the front page. As a result, important information, such as your personal details or qualifications, often gets pushed onto another page. The reader may never see them.

Many consultants and researchers ignore these pen portraits. Some even find them irritating. As we mentioned in Chapter Seven, what they want from your CV is relevant factual information, not your opinion of yourself.

Candidates often include pen portraits because they believe their CV needs to become a sales document. In our view a headhunter-friendly CV is purely factual. The *covering letter* is the sales document, as we will show in the next chapter.

In some cases candidates with perfectly good CVs receive a 'professional makeover', and end up with a completely different document. In the worst cases, CVs are transformed into tacky sales brochures. This will not do you any favours. In our experience, the strongest candidates with the most impressive CVs rarely include pen portraits. They let the facts speak for themselves, and allow search firms to decide if there is a potential fit with one of their assignments.

◆ Having gaps on your CV, which tend to arouse readers' suspicions. Sometimes there is a straightforward explanation, such as the time you spent travelling around Asia, looking for a suitable job or bringing up children. We even know of one candidate who was a 'human shield' during the first Gulf War, and spent several months being moved from one building to another until he was freed. Whatever happened, it is best to spell it out clearly on your CV.

◆ Using 'functional CVs', which group your work experience according to skills rather than listing them in chronological order. This format is often used to hide unexplained career gaps or other shortcomings, and search firms tend to be suspicious of them. Even if you have nothing to hide, a 'functional' CV is more difficult to skim quickly. It also makes your background much harder for the reader to piece together. As a result, your CV will be a prime candidate for the shredder!

We also recommend that you take care in the presentation of interim management or consultancy work. There is absolutely nothing wrong with either of these activities! However, some candidates try to hide interim assignments or disguise them as something else. Others use too much space on the front page describing assignments which lasted only a few weeks or months. Instead, we recommend you insert something like this:

2004–Present   Interim Management
                            3–6 month assignments in
                            manufacturing, retail and logistics

Many people believe that it is better to have a job when you contact the search firm. Some clients do seem to prefer candidates who are currently employed. However, in many cases confident and highly qualified candidates resign from well-paid positions and then approach search firms. They often feel that they have completed their task and want to move on. In other cases they no longer agree with the direction their company is taking.

The senior job market is much more fluid than it once was. It is now more acceptable to have a gap in your work experience, provided it is not too long and you have a good explanation.

Whatever you do, if you have already left your last job, do not pretend you are still there. Headhunters always check! Ultimately, consultants want a strong short list. If your experience matches the brief, it is likely to be irrelevant if you are currently employed or not. In fact, you may have an advantage if you are available to start work immediately.

(b) Your experience in detail

We can now move on to the second section of your CV, from page two onwards. This provides more detail regarding each of your jobs to date, including any interim assignments. An example is shown on page 76:

PROFESSIONAL EXPERIENCE

1983–1987   THE BIG ACCOUNTANCY FIRM

1983–1986   Audit Trainee
1986–1987   Audit Manager

I joined The Big Accountancy Firm straight from university, having received offers from several of the 'Big Eight' firms. My audit clients were privately-held and mid-cap companies in engineering, insurance, banking and business services.

I passed my professional examinations at the first attempt and was promoted to Audit Manager. My intention had always been to move out of the profession into industry. Within a year I was approached to join The Very Big Company as a Financial Analyst, and I accepted their offer.

1987–1994   THE VERY BIG COMPANY PLC

1987–1991   Financial Analyst
1991–1994   Head of Financial Accounting

The Very Big Company was the worldwide market leader in the production of high-performance widgets (HPWs), with revenues of £900m and a market capitalisation of £1bn. I was based at their Birmingham headquarters, where I reported to the Deputy Group Finance Director.

During this period my main responsibilities were as follows:

◆ Analysis of manufacturing costs, comparing plants in the UK, France and Taiwan. As a result, a decision was taken to close the French plant and concentrate production in the other two locations.

◆ Developing a financial model to evaluate a potential investment in a new production line. Using Net Present Value techniques, I concluded that the investment should proceed. The Board accepted my recommendation.

◆ Etc.

Just like the one-page summary, the second section should be factual and accurate. However, the aim of this section is different from the first. The research associate or consultant is sufficiently interested in your CV to have turned the page. What they now want is a clear description of your career to date, in order to decide whether to meet you.

The best format for each job is an introductory paragraph, and then a number of 'bullet points' setting out what you achieved in each role. Do mention the title, and perhaps even the name, of the person to whom you reported. It is also worth mentioning the titles of those who reported to *you*. This enables the reader to place you within the organisation. You can end with a sentence or two explaining why and how you left the job in question. If you meet the search consultant, you can then focus on the opportunity itself and explore how you might fit the specification. You are less likely to spend time explaining why you moved from company A to company B, etc.

You should also mention if one of the companies you worked for was sold, or merged with a subsequent employer. Some search consultants and clients make judgements about candidates based on the number of years between job moves. If you keep changing company every two years they may conclude that you never stay long enough for the results to catch up with you. You may therefore be regarded as unproven. However, if you are a high-flyer and your employer moves you to a different subsidiary every couple of years, then the story is completely different. It is important to display all of these jobs under an overall heading which gives the name of the *group* of companies for which you have worked.

One very good reason for using the format shown above is that it resembles the appraisal document commonly used by search firms. If the consultant is considering adding you to the short list and presenting you to the client, this format makes it much easier for them to do so. A typical appraisal document consists of a one-page summary followed by a few pages describing your experience in more detail. The third section is the consultant's evaluation of you in relation to the specification.

A final note about hobbies on your CV: consultants' views on them vary a great deal. If you do decide to mention your hobbies, we recommend you use the heading 'other interests', and are very selective. If you list too many of them, you risk giving the impression that your day job does not really interest you, so you seek fulfilment in other areas. A search firm is very unlikely to mention your hobbies to clients, although they may come up in a casual conversation between you and your prospective boss.

Above all, make sure your 'other interests' do not risk alienating your reader. Some headhunters love hunting, shooting and fishing. Others detest one or all of these activities. We once received a CV from a candidate who listed 'conversations with beautiful women' as one of his hobbies. This is probably not the best way of introducing yourself professionally!

Your Covering Letter

It is best to send your covering letter in the form of an e-mail, with your CV attached. If you send your letter as a second attachment, this will absorb more of the reader's time and slow things down. It is worth choosing a subject line which is both meaningful and clear.

SELLING YOURSELF

As we said in the last chapter, your covering letter is the sales document. Most consultants and researchers do not spend much time reading covering letters, and few attach them to their database. However, this is an opportunity to highlight your *unique selling proposition*. If you strike lucky, there will be a close fit between your USP and the Acid Test for a live assignment. You will be on the long list straightaway.

We recommend that you keep your letter short and to the point, making sure that vital information is also on your CV. If you want to change sectors, this is also the place to explain your motives and say why you think your experience is relevant to your future role.

Here is an example of a covering letter:

5 Elizabeth Close, Chester CH4 9YH

andrewsmith@xyz.com

Tel. 01244 000 000[1]

Ms A Hunter

Partner

Hyde & Seake

15 Curzon Avenue

London W1 2AB

Dear Ms Hunter[2]

I am writing to you on the recommendation of Martin Big[3], who tells me that you are one of the leading search consultants in the software sector.[4] I would be very grateful if you would consider me for any suitable assignments you may be handling.

Enclosed is my curriculum vitae. As you will see, for the past three years I have been VP Sales and Marketing – Europe with Scintillating Software, Inc.[5] My career goal is to become Chief Executive of a free-standing software company, either public or privately held.[6]

I believe I can offer your clients the following:[7]

◆ A 15-year track record in software, of which 10 have been in sales and marketing

◆ Experience of leading teams of up to 50 people, located throughout Europe

◆ An engineering degree from Birmingham University and an MBA from IMD in Switzerland

◆ Fluent French and a working knowledge of German[8]

For your information, my current salary is £140,000, with an on-target bonus of 50%.[9]

Thank you for your help. I look forward to hearing from you.[10]

Yours sincerely

Andrew Smith

Andrew Smith

It is worth discussing this step by step, so that you can apply the same principles to *your* covering letter:

1. You should include your contact details at the top of the page, just in case this letter becomes detached from your CV.

2. If you decide to send a printed letter, it is best to handwrite *Dear Ms Hunter*, or the equivalent, as it gives the letter a more personal touch. If you send a printed letter and CV, do send an electronic version in parallel, so that your CV can be attached to the database.

3. Mentioning a mutual friend or acquaintance gives you instant credibility, since you know some of the same people as Ms Hunter. The more senior this mutual contact, the better. As we explained in Chapter Four, Ms Hunter now has another reason to meet you: to be helpful towards Mr Big.

4. This shows that you have done your homework and understand which consultants specialise in your sector or job function. Again, you are a more credible candidate as a result: clearly not someone who is mail-merging letters from a directory!

5. Mentioning your current job on the front page should stimulate Ms Hunter's interest if she regularly recruits for software companies. Scintillating Software is well regarded and you are in a job function from which CEOs are often recruited.

6. You have told her exactly what you are looking for. This saves on guesswork and phone calls.

7. Please note the wording. You are suggesting that you have something to offer her clients. However, you have avoided appearing presumptuous. This is advisable since she probably knows her clients better than you do.

8. You have set out your unique selling proposition simply and clearly. The fact that you have given some thought to this can only make a good impression.

9. You have spared Ms Hunter and her colleagues the trouble of contacting you just to find out how much you earn. This will save them valuable time. It will also enable them to consider you as a candidate for an assignment straightaway.

10. You have left it up to her to contact you. Some search firms will acknowledge your approach by sending you a letter or an e-mail. However, unless you happen to fit one of their current assignments, there is no reason for them to speak to you right now. If they are interested in meeting you for one of the reasons we described in Chapter Four, they will be in touch. Otherwise, it is best not to call a consultant such as Ms Hunter, whom you do not already know. She may feel that you are wasting her time, which will not help you to build a relationship.

This covering letter is intended to be factual, but persuasive; no suggestion here that you are an 'entrepreneurial hands-on team-player'!

(10)

Some Tips on Presentation

Now that we have discussed the content of your CV and covering letter, it is time to talk about presentation. As in any marketing campaign, it pays to understand your potential customer's point of view.

Headhunters as a species are highly judgemental. In theory, only three judgements are required for them to be effective: (a) Can this candidate do an excellent job for our client? (b) Will they fit in? (c) Does this move make sense for them in career terms? In practice, search consultants tend to pass judgement on a far wider range of issues, from your written English to the way that you speak and dress. While some of these things are beyond the scope of this book, we can at least help you to avoid the obvious pitfalls when you draft your CV and write your covering letter.

In defence of search firms, there is some sense in using the quality of covering letters and CVs as a means of filtering candidates. If someone is applying for a senior position, but does not make the effort to write well, it is not an encouraging sign.

As in management consultancy and other professions, those who work in executive search are generally very well educated. A high proportion are arts graduates and used to writing well. Consultants and research associates have to produce their own documents to a high standard; they are likely to expect the same of you.

Many candidates put themselves at a disadvantage by making errors, which consultants and researchers are quick to spot. Some executives are so exalted in their organisations that no one dares to correct their grammar, spelling or use of English. They therefore make particular mistakes repeatedly. Others have worked for so long in their company or function that they have become incomprehensible to outsiders.

THINGS TO KEEP IN MIND

Here are a few points which you may find useful, all of them derived from the thousands of CVs which we have received.

Keep the format clean and simple

Spacing and layout make a big difference to the overall effect. Avoid cramming too much information onto each page. You will have enough space on page one if you have eliminated superfluous material such as the 'pen portrait' we discussed in Chapter Eight. You can then use two or three pages for the second section of your CV.

It is good to strike a balance between white space and text. Bullet points and intelligent spacing will help to break up the paragraphs. Choose a font which is easy to read or skim quickly. Your aim is to ensure that the reader keeps going and does not discard your CV immediately.

Understandably, many people do not ask their secretary, if they have one, to prepare their CV. However, home-made formatting is easy to spot. Unless you are particularly good at word-processing, we suggest you draft your CV as simply as possible and then ask an expert to improve the layout.

Avoid the top five pitfalls

Here are five common errors found in CVs and covering letters, and our suggestions for avoiding them:

'I would like to discuss my **future plans** with you.'
Presumably all plans relate to the future. Planning for the past would be rather odd. We recommend, 'I would like to discuss my plans with you'.

'The **current incumbent**'
The incumbent is *by definition* the person who currently holds a position. We recommend, 'The incumbent'.

'My **renumeration** package is as follows:'.
Correct: 'My remuneration package is as follows:'.

'I would like to **appraise** you of my situation'.
Correct: 'I would like to apprise you of my situation' or 'I would like to tell you about my situation.' The latter is clearer and less stilted.

'The company and **it's** strategy.'
It's is short for *it is*. The possessive pronoun is *its*, without an apostrophe.
Correct: 'The company and its strategy.'

Mind your Greek and Latin
One criterion, two criteria

He is an alumnus
She is an alumna
They are alumni
They are alumnae (if all are female)

Avoid using nouns as verbs
Example: 'I would like to leverage my finance skills in the IT sector.'

Leverage is a noun, but has been used here as a verb; the result is clumsy.

Better: 'I would like to apply my finance skills in the IT sector.'

Avoid shunting groups of adjectives and nouns together
This is a particularly common habit among those who have spent years working for certain large companies. As a test, try reading the following aloud, and making sense of it at the first attempt:

> I am an experienced private equity deal leader with a solid eight-year track record of appraising, completing and exiting over 40 successful development capital and change of control buy-out transactions in 15 European countries.

'Experienced private equity deal leader' is a mouthful because it consists of two adjectives followed by three nouns. This is also a long sentence, littered with expressions which are unfamiliar to most people. Your reader is much more likely to grasp what you are saying if you use more verbs and shorter sentences. We hope you will agree that this revised version is much clearer:

> I have considerable experience of leading transactions in private equity. Over the past eight years I have appraised, completed and sold over 40 investments in 15 European countries. These transactions have included (a) development capital and (b) buy-outs involving a change of control.

Spell out acronyms the first time you use them

Most organisations have their own terminology, including acronyms which save time and energy. However, these can often be misleading or incomprehensible, particularly to other nationalities. For example, *IRA* stands for Individual Retirement Account in the USA and Irish Republican Army in the UK. Similarly, *OBE* means not only Order of the British Empire (UK) but also Overtaken By Events (USA). As you can imagine, if you send a CV to an American with the heading *John Smith OBE*, you may not make the impression you intended. The obvious way to avoid confusion is to spell out acronyms in full the first time you use them.

Avoid split infinitives

The *infinitive* form of English verbs consists of two words, e.g. *to go, to walk, to run*, etc. There has been much controversy over whether it is acceptable to place an adverb between these two words.

Split infinitives are most common in the United States and in sectors such as IT where there is a strong American influence. However, many people – in the UK in particular – dislike split infinitives and consider them poor style. We therefore recommend that you avoid them. In many cases the adverb splitting the infinitive is actually redundant. For example, instead of writing 'I would like to briefly summarise my experience,' you can write 'I would like to summarise my experience.'

Be clear about currencies

If your CV is attached to a large search firm's database, it can be retrieved by any staff member in any office. It is therefore a good idea, when talking about money, to be absolutely clear about the currency.

Candidates often use the $ sign in their CVs and covering letters, leaving the reader to assume or guess which currency is meant. This can be confusing, particularly if the events you describe span several countries or continents. The $ sign refers to the local currency in a large number of countries across the globe. To avoid confusion, we recommend you write 'US$' to refer to amounts in US dollars. In other cases, it is probably best to write 'Australian dollars', for example, in the first instance and use 'AU$' thereafter.

Avoid sports metaphors and other expressions which may confuse the reader

Some Americans use a lot of terms from baseball and American football. Some British people are fond of cricket and rugby metaphors. Many people use expressions such as *heads-up* or *left-field* without knowing what they actually mean.

As ever, it is best to keep your readers in mind. Your CV and covering letter are likely to be read at some point by people who were educated in a different culture and/or who have no interest in sport. If in doubt, remove anything which could be confusing or unclear.

SOME TIPS FROM GEORGE

George Orwell, the essayist and author of *Animal Farm* and *Nineteen Eighty-Four*, was admired for the clarity of his prose. Here are his recommendations, from *Politics and the English Language*:

1. Never use a metaphor, simile or other figure of speech which you are used to seeing in print.

2. Never use a long word where a short one will do.

3. If it is possible to cut a word out, always cut it out.

4. Never use the passive when you can use the active.

5. Never use a foreign phrase, a scientific word, or a jargon word if you can think of an everyday English equivalent.

6. Break any of these rules sooner than say anything outright barbarous.

TEST MARKETING WILL IMPROVE YOUR CV AND COVERING LETTER

Once you are reasonably happy with your CV and covering letter, it is time to test them. First of all, we recommend that you ask a business-minded acquaintance to read what you have written. Another valuable test is to show your CV to someone who has no experience of business. The more easily they understand it, the better.

Proofread carefully

The final stage is proofreading. This is best carried out by you and a friend or relative who is a very critical reader and editor. Above all, do not rely on your computer's spell-checker. It is usually better to *print* the documents and read them at least twice.

Here is a sentence from one of the more alarming letters we have received:

> I would like to meet you, to discuss my skulls in more detail.

(11)

Conversations with Consultants

Your covering letter and CV will help you to build a relationship with the person most likely to consider you for an assignment, i.e. the consultant specialising in your sector or job function. If they do not have anything suitable, they may point you towards consultants in other firms who can help you directly.

In some cases the search consultant may decide to meet you. At the outset you should be clear about the context of the meeting; some candidates misjudge the situation. In Chapter Four we talked about the reasons why a search consultant might decide to meet you. The most likely reasons are that: (a) you are relevant to a current or impending assignment, and (b) the consultant is seeing you out of courtesy: perhaps you will be able to work with the firm in the future, as a candidate or client. Courtesy meetings tend to be brief, often lasting no more than 20 or 30 minutes.

You are most likely to meet in the consultant's office, but it could also be in a public place such as a hotel lobby or an airport. The important thing is to find a location within easy reach for both parties. It helps to be flexible about the time and venue, especially if the consultant is seeing you out of courtesy.

In any event, it is best to approach the meeting in a relaxed and open manner. Search consultants are human beings too, and will appreciate it if you make this part of their job as pleasant as possible.

WHAT *NOT* TO DO AT THE FIRST MEETING

The most common mistake is to treat the first meeting as a sales pitch. We have experienced this with a wide range of candidates, not only those who have worked in sales.

At one search firm we know, the receptionist had a habit of timing a particular consultant's courtesy interviews. The record was seven minutes, held by a candidate who arrived in the consultant's office, made his presentation, smiled, shook hands and left. This is an extreme case. However, it illustrates the point since everybody in that search team remembers the experience well, but not the name of the candidate. He made no attempt to build a relationship, and the meeting achieved nothing beyond general amusement.

On another occasion a consultant met a lady who had sent in her CV. She listened for a minute or so while he explained how the firm was structured and the kind of assignments they handled. Then she said, 'Why are you telling me this? I just want to know if there are any jobs going.' She also left within 10 minutes.

Experienced consultants have interviewed thousands of candidates, and quickly pick up signals from your behaviour.

Some things obviously do not go down well, such as trying too hard to impress, behaving arrogantly, and asking at the outset how much the job will pay.

If you have not been interviewed for a while, you may wish to consult a book on body language to help you to avoid certain habits. These include nervous tics and 'steepling': touching your hands together at the fingertips when speaking. This can be interpreted either as a sign that you feel superior or – confusingly – that you feel inferior. Neither will help you to build a rapport with the interviewer. Certain figures of speech are also best avoided. These include saying: 'to be honest'. This obviously raises questions about everything you have told the interviewer up to that point. Another distracting habit is 'upspeak': raising one's voice at the end of each sentence. Upspeak makes statements sound like questions, and can be very unsettling. It can also make you sound defensive.

We all have our habits and eccentricities. You can ask your partner, family members or friends to highlight any peculiarities in your speech or body language. They will often be happy to oblige!

Candidates who have spent years in the same organisation, with little recent interview practice, are the most likely to have picked up such habits. If you deal with most of your quirks before visiting a search firm, you will do yourself a big favour. Not all consultants have the time or the inclination to coach you, perhaps preferring to observe you in your natural state.

WHAT YOU *SHOULD* DO

It is a good idea to treat the first meeting with a search consultant as the start of a long-term business relationship. Ideally, the meeting should be relaxed and informal, with the candidate and the consultant both asking questions and exchanging information as they get to know each other.

We recommend that you dress appropriately. If you are in advertising, you are likely to dress differently from someone working in a bank, but it should be obvious that you are treating the meeting as a professional one. There may be a good reason for dressing differently, such as coming straight from work at a company which dresses down on Fridays. In this case you might not want to raise suspicions by going to your office in a suit. In any event, it is a good idea to warn the consultant or assistant of this when the meeting is set up. First impressions count.

It is essential to be on time for the meeting and to treat everyone you meet with courtesy. Quite a few consultants ask their assistant or the receptionist for their initial impression of the candidate, as they escorted him or her from the reception to the meeting room. Everything you say and do will contribute to the search firm's overall impression of you.

Most search consultants are sensitive to how well a candidate *listens*. It is often said that listening is more important than talking. We recommend that you listen carefully, and then follow up with a brief, but well-considered, question or statement.

If your CV is well written, there will be less need for detailed questions about the past. Instead, the meeting can focus on live issues, such as what you are looking for, and the assignments the firm is handling. If the consultant asks you to describe something in detail, it is still useful to ask at the end, 'Does that answer your question?' You will then know if you need to go any further.

Eye contact is also important. Some candidates barely look at the person they have just met, which raises a whole host of questions. Others try to maintain eye contact almost continuously. This can come across as artificial at best. If your eye contact is unrelenting, it can even be perceived as aggressive. It is usually better to re-establish eye contact at regular intervals.

Use the consultant's name sparingly. While most human beings feel more valued when they hear their name occasionally, it is best not to overdo this. Otherwise you risk giving the impression that you are desperate, and are trying too hard to please.

It is best to approach an interview with a search consultant as a meeting of peers or equals. They already know a lot about you, and this is your opportunity to find out more about them and their business. If you approach the interview in this way, you are likely to have a more relaxed and productive conversation, and make a more favourable impression.

STAY COOL
It is worth bearing in mind that quite a few assignments are cancelled. The industry average is that one in three search

assignments is never completed, even though the client has paid some or all of the fees. Some firms have much higher completion rates than this, which suggests that others do much worse. Cancellations can occur for a number of reasons, many of which are beyond the firm's control. For example, a reshuffle within the client organisation can make it unnecessary to recruit the new person after all.

Try not to be too frustrated about this. At least you have developed a relationship with the search consultant and their firm. This can only help you in future. If you accept the situation gracefully, they are likely to come back to you with another opportunity in due course.

Good search firms put lots of effort into building the long list and interviewing the most promising candidates. The consultant will test your skills and experience against the criteria agreed with the client. However, the decision to include you on the short list, or not, is ultimately an intuitive one.

The ideal short list consists of three to six candidates who would all do an excellent job, but who differ in terms of the balance of their skills and their personal style. The client can then choose the candidate who fits best. Sometimes it depends on the mixture of skills. At least as often, it is a question of 'chemistry': primarily the fit with the candidate's future boss.

Many candidates do not make it onto the short list simply because the consultant feels, intuitively, that the chemistry is not right. This comes partly from experience, including meeting thousands of candidates, and partly from a talent for anticipating who will fit with whom. The search consultant cannot be expected to predict how a candidate will perform in an interview with the client. However, some consultants are very good at screening out those who definitely *will not* fit.

Consultants express this in different ways. One of Britain's best-known search consultants asks the simple question, 'Can you see them together?' If the consultant knows both people well, there should be an intuitive response to this question.

There is only so much you can do to prepare for an interview. You can produce a first-rate covering letter and CV, and then get to know the search consultant and answer their questions. The rest is effectively out of your hands; you may as well relax and enjoy the process.

(12)

Interim Management

If you have jumped straight to this section, please note that our earlier chapters on CVs, covering letters and contacting search firms also apply to interim management!

Interim managers work on a temporary basis, to meet a company's short-term needs. This sector of recruitment first developed in the Netherlands during the 1970s. Boer & Croon, a management consultancy firm, was working on an assignment which then required a period of implementation. This was beyond their usual remit, so they looked for another solution. One possibility was to employ experienced managers to carry out the next phase. However, Dutch labour laws would have required redundancy payments at the end of the project. They eventually decided to hire some line managers on an interim basis. Thereafter, the firm kept a pool of experienced managers who could be engaged for a defined period when needed.

Interim management then expanded throughout Belgium, the Netherlands, the United Kingdom and Germany. The rest of Europe followed more slowly. It is now also established in Australasia.

In practice, the boundary between interim assignments and permanent employment is blurred. An interim appointment can last from one month to two years or more, while a 'permanent' role usually lasts at least a year. In a very small number of cases the interim manager will subsequently accept a full-time job with the client.

WHY DO COMPANIES WANT AN INTERIM SOLUTION?

There are two main reasons why a client may want an interim manager:

1. There is a gap in their management team which needs to be filled urgently. This can arise for a number of reasons, such as illness or a sudden resignation. The presence of an interim manager allows business to continue as usual.

2. They need a specialist to complete a particular project or to achieve a certain result. Maybe the company has acquired a new subsidiary. Equally, there may be a crisis, such as a business which needs to be turned around.

One solution would be to reassign an executive from elsewhere in the organisation. However, there is frequently no one available with the skills needed. For the second category of assignment, the company could hire a management consultant from one of the well-known firms. However, this can be very expensive and some clients fear there will be more emphasis on analysis than implementation.

There are several advantages to hiring an interim manager:

1. They are usually highly experienced, verging on over-qualified. They will have carried out this task, or a similar one, at least once before.

2. They tend not to get involved in the client company's politics. Their focus is on solving the problem and then moving on to a new project.

3. They are usually cheaper than consultants, even when the intermediary's fees are included in the calculation.

4. Interim contracts can be terminated at any time, usually at one month's notice on either side. Hence they are a variable cost rather than a fixed one.

5. Interim managers are not generally included in the headcount. This can be important if a hiring freeze has been imposed or an organisation is making people redundant.

THE STRUCTURE OF THE INTERIM MARKET

The most common way for candidates to win interim assignments is via their personal networks. This happens roughly 70 per cent of the time. If you are available for interim work, it is quite possible that a former boss or colleague will employ you on a short-term basis.

The other 30 per cent of assignments are accounted for by recruitment businesses which focus on providing clients with interim managers. Some of these are specialist practices within large search firms, providing obvious synergies with the firms' other search activities. For example, a client may engage a search firm to find a new managing director for a particular division. The assignment will ideally be completed in 90 days. However, there may also be a notice period or 'gardening leave' which prevents the successful candidate from joining for several months. The client may decide to hire an interim who will fill the gap in the meantime.

Other interim management businesses are independent. They either win their assignments on the open market, or serve clients referred to them by other professional advisors.

In the UK there are some 300 intermediaries offering interim managers, operating at various levels. Here are some of the firms serving the top end of the market:

Name	Website
Ballantyne (part of Highland Partners Ltd)	www.ballantyne.highlandsearch.com
BIE Interim Executive	www.bieinterim.com
Boyden	www.boyden.com
Executive Interim Management (EIM)	www.eim.com
Heidrick & Struggles Interim Executives	www.heidrick.com
Odgers Interim	www.odgers.com

Some areas within interim management are more active than others. There tends to be a particularly strong demand for finance directors and general managers, for example. There are also regular requests for specialists in strategy and information technology.

During an economic downturn there are large numbers of potential candidates, and new interim firms also tend to spring up. Some of them are sole traders who know a few unemployed executives and begin approaching corporate clients on their behalf. However, as in mainstream executive search, the leading interim management firms tend to have strong brands based on a consistent, high-quality service. This helps them to attract the best candidates and to generate repeat business from clients. The firms are usually small, so it is frequently the individual consultant's reputation which counts.

HOW MUCH WILL YOU EARN?

A common rule of thumb is that interim managers charge a day rate equal to a maximum of one per cent of their previous base salary. The higher your base salary, the more difficult it is to achieve one per cent. The exception to this rule is those earning more than £200,000 for turning around businesses in distress. These company doctors can often earn more than one per cent per day, once performance bonuses are taken into account.

Your day rate should leave a margin to cover additional costs, holidays and breaks between assignments which you may need to devote to marketing your services. Of course, your actual day rate will be determined by market conditions, i.e. the scarcity of your skills.

HOW IS THE REMUNERATION STRUCTURED?

As elsewhere in executive search, the interim management firm usually charges the client one third of the daily rate received by the candidate. However, some firms will opportunistically charge more than this. Some interim firms pay the candidates themselves, and then invoice their clients for the same daily rate, plus one-third. In other words, they add a fee of 33 per cent and take full responsibility for collecting the money from the client. In other cases, the candidate invoices the client directly, and the interim firm invoices the client separately in order to collect its fee.

In both cases it is common for the candidate to operate via a service company. This is a limited company which undertakes assignments for several different clients. If you choose this option it is essential to comply with the relevant legislation, especially regarding tax and National Insurance contributions. In the UK it is particularly important to comply with the legislation known as 'IR35'.[4]

Many interim firms charge one-third of the placed candidate's day rate for as long as the candidate continues to work for the client. Often the percentage fee is reduced or capped after one or two years. However, this condition varies a great deal from one firm to another. In some cases the firm charges an additional fee. This can be up to one-third of first-year cash remuneration if the interim becomes a permanent employee.

---

[4] See the Inland Revenue's website at www.inlandrevenue.gov.uk

HOW WILL INTERIM MANAGEMENT FIT WITH YOUR LONGER-TERM CAREER?

Some candidates make a positive decision to become an interim manager, often because they are attracted to the lifestyle. They can earn as much as (or more than) they did when they were employed, while only working for part of the year, with time to pursue other interests. Some like to undertake projects overseas and relocate for a few months, particularly if it suits their lifestyle and family situation.

Other candidates find themselves in interim management by default, during a downturn in the market for permanent employment. They take on interim assignments while waiting for the economy to pick up again. Many of them discover that they like the lifestyle and the role of an interim, and they decide to continue.

Unsurprisingly, downturns greatly increase the supply of candidates, and depress the day rates for interim work. However, this does not usually apply to the top level, where there is a limited supply of really good people to lead major change programmes. Some candidates continue to earn very high day rates, even in the depths of a recession, because their particular skills are in high demand. For example, if a client is saving millions by restructuring or closing down a particular operation, the cost of a top-quality interim is small in comparison.

WHAT ARE THE PROS AND CONS OF INTERIM MANAGEMENT?

In some cases an interim assignment can give you experience of another sector, and help your career to move in that direction. You may be offered a permanent role with the client company once they get to know you.

On the other hand, it can be hard to develop professionally if clients employ you for something you have done before. You may then keep carrying out similar projects in the same industry. However, interim executives often say that they learn a lot from each assignment, even if it is in an area that they know well.

DECLARING YOUR INTEREST IN INTERIM MANAGEMENT

You can mention in your covering letter that you are prepared to consider interim assignments as well as permanent roles. However, some candidates are concerned that once they begin working as an interim they will be labelled as such, and become less marketable for permanent appointments.

It is true that some search consultants used to regard interim management as the preserve of people who had reached a plateau with their former employer. However, nowadays some very talented executives spend part of their careers in interim management. For many of them, the objective is to find work that they want to do, without worrying about whether it is labelled as 'interim', 'fixed contract', 'consulting' or 'permanent'.

If you do take on an interim assignment, it is best to keep some time available for interviews with longer-term employers. Clients often appreciate that interims have to market themselves, and you can therefore negotiate a certain number of days off to look for your next interim assignment. Naturally they do not pay for this! Some interim managers also have non-executive directorships, to which they dedicate a certain number of days on a regular basis.

SEARCHES FOR INTERIM MANAGERS TEND TO BE QUICK

Searches for interim managers are usually completed more quickly than those for permanent staff, often within a few days. Otherwise there would not be much point! One reason for this is that the firm usually knows some qualified candidates at the outset. The aim is to assemble a short list quickly. Candidates usually start straightaway because they are available for work and do not need to relocate their families.

Apart from this streamlined approach, the process tends to be very similar to a standard search assignment. You are likely to be contacted by phone and then interviewed if appropriate. Appraisal documents may be more concise, since the aim is to meet a short-term need rather than ensure a good long-term fit. The client is likely to meet fewer candidates before deciding: usually two or three.

In conclusion, interim management has many advantages, as both a short- and long-term career option. In either case, while you are working on an interim assignment it is important to stay in touch with other potential users of your services.

(13)

Becoming a Non-Executive Director

Non-executive directors can be divided into two main categories. There are those with a full-time job who also sit on the boards of one or more other companies. The second group consists of retired executives who build a portfolio of non-executive directorships, maybe five or more. This is sometimes described as 'going plural', and can become a full-time activity. Your approach to becoming a non-executive should largely be determined by whether you belong to the first or the second category.

WHY DO YOU WANT TO DO IT?

The motivation for an executive to join the board of another company often includes career development. A managing director in the brewing industry might, for example, sit on the board of an IT company to gain broader business experience. A better understanding of the IT sector may also be valuable in his or her executive role.

Those who are progressing through the ranks of a large company may become non-executive directors of smaller quoted companies to gain experience of corporate govern-ance and other shareholder issues. This can help them to reach the board of the larger company which employs them. In some cases large companies encourage their rising stars to broaden their experience in this way.

In order for you to become a non-executive director, it is a requirement that there should be no conflict of interest with your day job. In the example above you might wish to consider whether the non-executive role would cause a problem if you subsequently moved into the IT sector.

Unless you have already gone plural, you are likely to obtain a better non-executive position if you are in full-time employment. If you are looking for a job it is usually better to focus on that, rather than exploring non-executive roles at the same time.

There is now an established and growing population of full-time non-executive directors, many of whom have been senior executives, venture capitalists, bankers or other professionals. Clients may require that newcomers to the board should have gone plural, so that they have the flexibility to dedicate extra time to the company when required.

Some people now switch to a non-executive career in their forties or fifties, often as chairman of one or more companies. Companies are also keen to find non-executives who could join the committees responsible for audit, nominations or remuneration. One common reason for going plural is to establish a better balance between work and other activities including family commitments. Another is to embark on a new career whilst employing your existing skills.

WILL YOU BE ANY GOOD AT IT?

Being a non-executive director requires different skills from those of an executive, although there is some overlap. A frequent complaint about executives who join the board of another company is that they do not act in an advisory capacity, tending to assert themselves as though they were running the business. This is obviously a question of personality, as some executives make the transition perfectly well.

Some finance directors, who have spent years supporting their chief executives, find the transition to a non-executive role straightforward. A financial training which emphasises the need to act in shareholders' interests also helps. However, this habit of playing a supporting role can also hold them back. Some are criticised for not contributing enough to debates on strategy and commercial decision-making.

THE DEMANDS ON NON-EXECUTIVES ARE INCREASING

Non-executive appointments often used to be the preserve of company chairmen who asked each other to join their respective boards. The role was not very demanding; in the worst cases, non-executives turned up for a nice lunch and a board meeting, contributing little.

However, the situation has changed rapidly in recent years, as corporate governance rules have become progressively more demanding on both sides of the Atlantic. This trend has been driven by regulators, such as the Financial Services

Authority and the London Stock Exchange. In the UK, there have been various reports, produced by committees named after their chairmen, such as Cadbury (1992), Greenbury (1995), Hampel (1998) and Higgs (2003). These committees' recommendations have then been incorporated into *The Combined Code on Corporate Governance*, published by the Financial Services Authority. The 2003 edition draws on both the Higgs Report, which reviewed the role and effectiveness of non-executive directors, and on the review of audit committees led by Sir Robert Smith.[5]

It is important to note that the law does not differentiate between executive and non-executive directors. All are simply viewed as directors, with the same responsibilities. The Higgs Report contains a 'Pre-Appointment Due Diligence Checklist for New Board Members' that includes questions you should ask before joining a board.[6]

The year 2000 saw the start of a bear market in equities in which failures of corporate governance helped to depress share prices. A spate of accounting scandals, particularly in the United States, accelerated the wave of new legislation intended to prevent such things ever occurring again. There have been two particularly important themes. The first is a desire to make directors responsible for the integrity of financial reporting to investors. The second is a greater emphasis on the role of non-executive directors in monitoring the conduct of executives.

---

[5] See the Financial Services Authority's website at www.fsa.gov.uk/pubs: Combined Code, The Smith Report.
[6] Se the Department of Trade and Industry's website at www.dti.gov.uk/cld/non_exec_review

The Higgs Report made a number of recommendations which have increased the demand for non-executives. Companies are expected either to comply with the recommendations or to explain why they have not done so.

The first recommendation was that at least half the members of the board, excluding the chairman, should be *independent* non-executives. The Combined Code only requires this of the largest 350 quoted companies, as measured by market capitalisation. However, it recommends that a smaller company should have at least *two* independent non-executives. The second point is that the roles of the chairman and the chief executive should be performed by separate people. Thirdly, the chief executive should not become chairman of the same company.

It is far from certain that more rules produce better-run companies. However, recent developments *have* increased the demands placed on non-executives, in terms of time, attention to detail, and the need to show that the principles of good corporate governance have been adhered to. In the UK, the risk of being sued by disgruntled shareholders has also risen, although insurance can mitigate the financial exposure to some extent.

THE ROLE OF THE NON-EXECUTIVE DEPENDS ON THE SIZE OF THE COMPANY

As a general rule, smaller companies often look to their non-executives to provide skills which the executive team does not possess. An obvious example would be a privately held but fast-growing technology company with founders in their twenties. They might look for non-executive directors to help them with fundraising and winning business at a senior level. Similarly, small quoted companies often have a small management team whose skills do not cover all eventualities. They may therefore appoint a non-executive director with skills in mergers and acquisitions, technology or a particular market which is important to the company.

Among the larger companies, particularly in the FTSE 100, non-executive appointments are often required to convince institutional investors that the business is in safe hands. There is a premium on candidates with substantial experience on the boards of large public companies. Fund managers have become much more willing to veto the appointment of candidates they do not like, and accelerate the departure of board members who they feel are not performing.

CHICKENS AND EGGS

The conundrum for many candidates may be summarised as follows: 'You can't join a board because you haven't been on a board before'. In other words, if you have not reached the board of a public company in your executive career, it is hard to be appointed to such a board in a non-executive capacity.

However, there are ways around this problem. If the board particularly wants to attract someone with your background as a non-executive director, then you have a better chance. Another solution is to contribute a skill which the company badly needs. Your executive role may also be in an industry which offers useful parallels with the client company's business.

Some people use the boards of private companies as stepping stones to the boards of public ones. Once you have gained experience as a non-executive of a private company, it is easier to make the transition to a public one. If your company lists on a stock exchange, then it may happen automatically.

Others prefer to stick to private companies, saying that the work is more varied and less restricted by stock exchange reporting requirements. If you are planning a career as a non-executive, it can be a good idea to have a board seat with a good quoted company, even if the rest of your activities are with privately-held businesses.

HOW MUCH WILL YOU EARN?

The annual reports of publicly quoted UK companies state all directors' remuneration. Historically, non-executives have not been very well paid, particularly in relation to their day jobs. Salient exceptions are the chairmen of some large public companies.

However, the fees paid to non-executives in the UK have been rising, as the role itself has become more demanding. One large public company even trebled its non-executive directors' fees, apparently for this reason, shortly after the Higgs Report was published. However, some remuneration consultants believe that the effective *hourly rate* has remained the same, or has even fallen slightly, as non-executives are required to work harder than ever.

In some cases non-executives have been rewarded with share options, which can be lucrative. However, critics argue that this undermines their impartiality and can jeopardise financial reporting standards. Will non-executives resist aggressive accounting policies which boost reported earnings if they stand to gain from any increase in the share price?

Directors may also be paid an agreed rate for additional responsibilities on the board. There is usually a flat fee for membership, or chairmanship, of the audit committee or the committees responsible for appointments and remuneration.

If you want to make real money, it may be better to be an angel investor. These invest some cash and a lot of hard work, in return for an equity stake in a fast-growing company. In this case you may not need to be a non-executive director at all, at least in the formal sense. Particularly in the technology sector, angels tend to join an *advisory board*, where they work alongside the chief executive and other members of the executive team. It is important to note that they also take far higher financial risks than most non-executives, since they invest their own cash in the business.

If you have a strong track record as an executive in a particular sector, you may have the opportunity to chair a company backed by angels, venture capital or private equity. Financial packages for such chairmen often combine cash and equity. Part of your role will be to act as a buffer between the investors and the executives running the company. The number of such roles has increased in recent years.

You should obviously seek independent legal advice before becoming either a non-executive director or a member of an advisory board. Even if you are a member of an advisory board, there is still a chance that you will be regarded as a 'shadow director', with similar legal liabilities, if the company gets into difficulty.

WHY ARE SEARCH FIRMS INTERESTED IN NON-EXECUTIVE APPOINTMENTS?

Search firms have been involved in the appointment of non-executives for many years. The increased emphasis on corporate governance has made it more necessary than ever to show that board appointments have been scrutinised. One way of doing this is to appoint a search firm which will evaluate candidates impartially.

In large search firms the team that recruits non-executives is often referred to as the 'Board Practice'. It is certainly very interesting for search consultants to work with, and place, senior people on the boards of well-known companies. From the search firm's point of view, non-executive assignments are also an excellent marketing activity. Most, if not all, of the candidates on a short list will be potential clients, since they usually occupy senior positions in other companies.

Business people, like most other human beings, prefer to work with those they know and trust. They will often engage a search firm which has placed them elsewhere as an executive or non-executive, or has even presented them as a candidate without success. Candidates who feel good about the way they have been treated are likely to consider the same search firm for their own assignments.

A search firm will often seek to be active in both executive and non-executive assignments. If the firm places a chairman, then it may be asked to find other members of the board, perhaps including the chief executive. If it has brought in the chief executive, then it may be asked to recruit his or her direct reports. If the firm is active in recruiting executives, this should in turn give it a better knowledge of the rising stars who will make good candidates for non-executive roles with other companies. It then becomes a virtuous circle.

HOW DO SEARCH FIRMS LOOK FOR NON-EXECUTIVES?

As mentioned above, in the not-so-distant past non-executive appointments were largely the preserve of the chairman or even the chief executive. Some companies later decided to appoint a search firm to manage the recruitment process. However, the search firm often still drew its candidates from a limited pool.

Cynics sometimes suggest that this pool consisted largely of the search firm's other clients, who needed to be rewarded for their generosity in hiring the firm to carry out searches for executives. Institutional shareholders have become increasingly sensitive to this.

A more charitable interpretation would be that search firms often limit themselves to candidates who are already directors of other companies, particularly quoted ones. The candidate pool is then conveniently reduced to directors who can be researched relatively easily using information which is in the public domain.

Increasingly however, companies look for non-executives in much the same way as they look for executives. A search firm is appointed, in-depth research is carried out, and a long list is drawn up which is then distilled into a short list.

FIND THE CONSULTANTS WHO SPECIALISE IN NON-EXECUTIVE APPOINTMENTS

The process for finding consultants who specialise in non-executives is no different than the one we described for executive roles within a certain sector or function. As we said in Chapter Three, it is best to look at search firms' websites, consult publications and ask people you know to make recommendations. It is also worth calling the switchboard to check that whoever is listed is still with the firm!

There is no standard structure for handling non-executive assignments. In some firms it is the most senior, or the oldest, consultants who focus on non-executives. One reason for this is that their peers may be on the boards of many companies, particularly as chairmen.

In other firms the heads of the practices specialising in a sector or function handle non-executive searches. Collectively, they form the 'board practice'. If the client wants a new board member with a background in consumer products or finance, for example, then the practice heads should have the best knowledge of the candidate pools in question.

In conclusion, becoming a non-executive director is *not* a soft option. Neither is it a stop-gap between jobs. It can be very rewarding, and can extend your career by several years.

It can also help you to strike a better balance between work and other areas of your life.

(14)

Keeping in Touch

Those who cultivate relationships with the appropriate search consultants are more likely to be contacted for an assignment. It is a good idea to start doing this while you are still employed. However, if you are currently 'between jobs' then you have the time and flexibility to meet a larger number of consultants. Any contacts you establish now could last you many years and help to carry you through several job moves.

Whatever your starting point, it pays to be systematic about building your network of contacts among the search firms. As we mentioned earlier, some consultants will refer you to their counterparts in other firms. If they do, it is good to follow up with an e-mail telling them how you got on, and which consultants have been helpful.

DEVELOPING YOUR RELATIONSHIP WITH SEARCH FIRMS

This is how you can maintain and develop your relationship with search firms:

♦ Be a good source. Do your best to help research associates and consultants whenever they ask you for advice.

◆ If your CV has changed since you were last in touch, send an updated version to the firms which are most likely to have an opportunity for you.

◆ Return calls swiftly and behave professionally, even if you are not interested in a particular opportunity.

◆ Give the search consultant feedback, by e-mail, if you have been in touch with someone they have recommended.

◆ Meet face to face occasionally if the consultant has the time and the inclination. If it feels appropriate, send an e-mail afterwards to say thank you.

◆ Don't be a nuisance! There is no need to remind the search firm of your existence by calling at regular intervals. If you are well-documented and have a good reputation, the firm will call you as soon as it has a suitable assignment.

All of the above will greatly improve the quantity and quality of the approaches you receive. We hope that this book helps you to build your relationships with search firms, and find exciting opportunities.

Good luck with your search!

John Purkiss
Barbara Edlmair

Further information on John Purkiss and Barbara Edlmair is at www.johnpurkiss.com

Index

If you want to know how . . . to build brilliant
business connections

'Brilliant Business Connections are what everyone
who wants to succeed in business really needs. But
how do you make them and what should you do to get
the most from them?

'Whatever your level of expertise, you will find
common sense tips, advice and suggestions on how to
build your own personal network of connections.
Armed with this knowledge you will have greater
confidence and progress further and faster with your
career and building your business. You will also
probably have more fun too!'

Frances Kay

Brilliant Business Connections
How powerful networking can transform you and
your company's performance
Frances Kay

Frances Kay – author, businesswoman and
professional coach – guides you through the intricate
steps of professional and personal relationship
building. She tells you how the top people do it;

- externally for business development;

- internally for positive staff relationships and
  proactive teams; and

- personally for a brilliant social life.

ISBN 1 85703 969 6

If you want to know how ... to present with power

'Your ability to communicate is the single most important factor in your professional tool bag. People who make a difference, who inspire others, who get promoted, are usually excellent communicators. The people who have shaped the course of history were all excellent communicators. They could move audiences, win minds and hearts and get people to take action.

'The need to communicate is even greater in today's fast-changing workplace. Of all the ways you communicate, the one that gives you the greatest chance to make a powerful impact is the presentation.

'This book covers all you need to know about researching your material, structuring your message and designing your visual aids, it also shows you ways to develop confidence and gives tips on how to deliver. Whether you are a novice speaker or a seasoned pro, this book will give you tips and techniques that will take you to the next level.'

Shay McConnon

Presenting with Power
Captivate, motivate, inspire and persuade
Shay McConnon

'Shay's raw talent together with his passion for the audience and his material make for a magical experience.' – *Siemens*

'His engaging style of presentation ... captivates his audience whatever their background or current state of motivation.' – *Director, Walkers Snack Foods*

ISBN 1 84528 022 9

If you want to know how . . . to write a report

'In this book you will learn how to write reports that will be read without unnecessary delay; understood without undue effort; accepted and, where applicable, acted upon. To achieve these aims you must do more than present all the relevant facts accurately, you must also communicate in a way that is both acceptable and intelligible to your readers.'

John Bowden

Writing a Report

How to prepare, write and present effective reports
John Bowden

'What is special about the text is that it is more than just how to "write reports"; it gives that extra really powerful information that can, and often does, make a difference. It is by far the most informative text covering report writing that I have seen . . . This book would be a valuable resource to any practising manager.' – *Training Journal*

'With the help of this sensible step-by-step guide, anybody can develop first-rate report writing skills.' – *Building Engineer*

ISBN 1 85703 922 X

If you want to know how . . . to write a senior level CV

'Competition in the job market for senior and professional roles is increasingly fierce, and your CV is a vital tool in winning the post that you want. Most job advertisements attract many more applicants than could possibly be interviewed. If your CV stands out from the rest – if the recruiter can see at a glance that you have just what their company needs – your chances of getting an interview are very much higher.'

Rachel Bishop-Firth

The Ultimate CV for Managers and Professionals
Win senior managerial positions with an outstanding resumé
Rachel Bishop-Firth

'A thoroughly clear and admirably concise guide.' – *www.newmonday.com*

'I was impressed by the eye-catching and professional layouts suggested by the author and by useful advice on how to write the covering letter so that it grips the reader's attention.' – *Focus on Business Education*

ISBN 1 85703 995 5

If you want to know how . . . to prepare for interviews

'It's the interviewer's prerogative to throw just about any question they can think of at the interviewee. So you might think that it's almost impossible to prepare for an interview. But the truth is that 80% of interview questions revolve around 20 common themes. And many interviewees let themselves down by not thinking about these themes, preparing and rehearsing responses to them.

'Many candidates then go on to create a wrong impression. Remember that an interviewer has to like you and warm to you as a person, as well as want to work with you because you answer the questions well. I see too many candidates who talk too much or come across as nervous or unfriendly. If you get the chance to rehearse with a friend and get some feedback on just how you come across, you will improve your chances no end.'

Rob Yeung

Successful Interviews – Every Time
Rob Yeung

'Successful Interviews is the type of book that one may not wish to share with others who are job seeking in competition with oneself. Nevertheless, I owe a debt of gratitude to Dr Rob Yeung for sharing his experiences with us . . .' – *S. Lewis, Coventry*

'This book is an invaluable source of information for job hunters on preparing for interviews, tests and assessment centres.' – *Jonathan Turpin, Chief Executive of job hunting website fish4jobs.co.uk*

ISBN 1 85703 978 5

If you want to know how . . . to handle tough
job interviews

'Job interviews can be daunting, because often there is
our livelihood at stake. A little preparation and
understanding about how interviews work can help.
Even better is understanding the purpose of the
different stages of interview in a recruitment process,
and the balance of power in those interviews.

'This book is about understanding why you are there,
and what to do when things get difficult. It's about
knowing your way through the recruitment process so
that each hurdle is cleared to get you the job you want
– if it's right for you.'

Julie-Ann Amos

Handling Tough Job Interviews
Be prepared, perform well, get the job
Julie-Ann Amos

'A wealth of sound advice.' – *Sesame (Open
University magazine)*

'Takes you step-by-step through the recruitment
process and gives useful advice on interviews with
senior management, dealing with psychometric tests;
and discussing and agreeing the job offer.' – *Office
Secretary*

'Its strength is that it covers all kinds of interview
from recruitment agencies and headhunters to
employer and human resources.' – *Phoenix Magazine*

ISBN 1 85703 845 2

If you want to know how . . . to excel at psychometric and assessment tests

'The good news is there are thousands of brilliant firms out there offering everything from sky-high salaries, profit-related bonuses, long holidays, flexible working, staff discounts, free shares, free canteens, health and life insurance, advanced training, gyms, outings, holidays . . . not to mention the job satisfaction and level of responsibility you've always known you could handle. But the reality is that the days when all you needed to land a top job was a great CV and a sparkling performance at interview are long gone. Now you must also pass a whole range of psychometric and management tests with flying colours. And that's exactly what this book is here to help you to do.'

Andrea Shavick

Management Level Psychometric & Assessment Tests
Everything you need to help you land that senior job
Andrea Shavick

Whether you're after a junior management, senior management or even director level position, or simply want to familiarise yourself with the very latest selection and recruitment techniques this book will meet your needs. It includes:

- 35 genuine management levels practice psychometric tests and a guide to online testing.
- Everything you need to know about personality questionnaires, plus loads of practice material.
- A complete guide to what to expect and how to survive an assessment centre visit.
- Detailed information on high-level assessment centre exercises commonly used to test candidates.
- A guide to researching your chosen organisation.

ISBN 1 84528 028 8

How To Books are available through all good bookshops, or you can order direct from us through Grantham Book Services.

Tel: +44 (0)1476 541080
Fax: +44 (0)1476 541061
Email: orders@gbs.tbs-ltd.co.uk

Or via our website

www.howtobooks.co.uk

To order via any of these methods please quote the title(s) of the book(s) and your credit card number together with its expiry date.

For further information about our books and catalogue, please contact:

**How To Books
3 Newtec Place
Magdalen Road
Oxford OX4 1RE**

Visit our web site at

www.howtobooks.co.uk

Or you can contact us by email at

info@howtobooks.co.uk